CW00922911

Battle of Britain over Kent

Bitter Harvest

Volume 1: May / August 1940

By Paul Nash

Published by Paul Nash

Copyright © Paul Nash

ISBN 978-0-9559444-2-0

Printed and bound by CPI Group (UK) Ltd, Croydon, CR0 4YY

Bitter Harvest - Volume 1: June/August 1940

Table of Contents

Glossary & abbreviations

Cover artwork: Thanks to my gifted and artistic brother, Robin, for improving my amateurish efforts.

Front cover photo: After attacking Kenley airfield on the 3rd of July 1940, this Dornier Do 17 Z from the 8th *Staffel* / KG 77 was intercepted and shot down by Hurricanes. The bullet-riddled remains came to rest in hop fields at Paddock Wood, near Tonbridge. (Via Red Kite Books)

Abteilung 5

This was the *Luftwaffe's* intelligence department.

Abwehrkreis

Formations of *Messerschmitt Bf 110* heavy fighters and fighter-bombers would frequently adopt this formation over southern England in which the individual aircraft of the formation flew in a circle with each aircraft covering the aircraft in front. Often called a defensive circle, it was frequently used for this purpose later in the summer when the heavy aircraft were under attack from more nimble, single engine fighters. It was also used in the early days of the battle, since the spectacle of a *staffel* or *gruppe* of these aircraft circling overhead was very visible. It was intended as an attempt to lure British fighters into the air in an effort to neutralise RAF fighter command's strength.

Adlerangriff (Eagle Attack)

This was the code name for the *Luftwaffe's* air assault against Britain in 1940.

Adlertag (Eagle Day)

This was the code name for the first day of the *Luftwaffe's* air assault against Britain in 1940.

AOC

Air Officer Commanding was the title for the officer in charge of individual RAF Fighter Command Group areas.

Bf

For the sake of simplicity, the two fighters (109 and 110) manufactured and supplied to the *Luftwaffe* during the Battle of Britain by *Messerschmitt* are shown with their model numbers prefixed by *Bf*, short for *Bayerische Flugzeugwerke*. There was a complicated chain of model ownership between *Messerchmitt Flugzeugbau*, *Bayerische Flugzeugwerke* and *Messerschmitt AG*, Willy Messerschmitt's own company. It's common for all *Messerschmitt* aircraft of this period to be referred to with the *Me* prefix before the model number, but it seems more likely that both the 109 and the 110 models should have the *Bf* prefix and all later models the *Me* prefix, e.g. *Me 210/410/163/262*, etc.

Bordfunker

This was the *Luftwaffe* term describing the role of radio operator/gunner, particularly commonplace for the second crew member in the crews of *Messerschmitt Bf 110* heavy fighters and Stuka dive-bombers of the period.

British Expeditionary Force (BEF)

British Army and RAF units assisting the defence of Belgium, Holland and France.

Chain-home

This was the term describing the series of radar sites located around the coast of Britain, with the only gaps being in the northwest of Scotland, the Bristol Channel and a portion of the Welsh coast. There were 21 sites (CH) designed to identify formations at high altitude at the start of the Battle of Britain, and a further 30 sites (CHL) designed to identify formations at low level or shipping.

Der schwarze Donnerstag

This was the German term for the 15th of August 1940, when the *Luftwaffe* and the RAF suffered their heaviest losses during the summer of 1940.

Erprobungsgruppe

Operational test wing dedicated to trials of new aircraft or tactics in front line service. *Erprobungsgruppe 210* was the most prominent unit that used this title during the summer of 1940.

Experten

The *Luftwaffe* gave this title to pilots who had five confirmed aerial victories to their name. It's similar to the "ace" term used by the Allies.

Feldwebel (Fw)

This was broadly equivalent to Flight Sergeant in the RAF.

Freie Jagd

This term applied to the offensive sorties conducted by German fighter units, frequently with no specific target laid down, but generally aimed at enticing British fighters up from their airfields so they could be engaged and destroyed.

Generalfeldmarschall

In recognition of their contribution to the victories that Germany had won since the autumn of 1939, Hitler promoted both Kesserling and Sperrle to the rank of *Generalfeldmarschall*. This was a rank broadly equivalent to Marshall of the Royal Air Force.

Geschwader

This was broadly equivalent in aircraft numbers to a Group in the RAF. There would normally be a Headquarters' Flight of 3-4 aircraft as the *Geschwaderstab*, with at least three *Gruppen*, each with their own Headquarters' flight of 3-4 aircraft together with three *Staffeln* of 13-15 aircraft. At full operational strength, the *Geschwader* would have some 150 aircraft.

Geschwaderkommodore

This was the commander of a Group within the *Luftwaffe*, applicable for both fighters and bombers, broadly equivalent to a Group Captain in the RAF.

Gruppe(n)

Roughly equivalent in aircraft numbers to a Wing in the RAF, there were normally three *Gruppen* to each *Geschwader*, each with a complement of 40 -

45 aircraft, although this was frequently smaller or larger, according to operational requirements and losses. Each *Gruppe* was subdivided into three *Staffeln*, as well as a small headquarters' (*Stab*) flight. The *Gruppe* number was always shown as a Roman numeral.

Gruppenkommandeur

This was the rank given to the leader of a *Gruppe*, which was broadly equivalent to the rank of Wing Commander in the RAF in terms of the numbers of aircraft controlled. He would normally hold the rank of *Major* or *Oberst.*

Hardest Day

The 18th of August 1940 saw both sides of the conflict suffering heavy losses and became known by this term.

Hauptmann

This was broadly equivalent to a Flight Lieutenant in the RAF.

Idiotenreihen

This was the term used by German fighter pilots viewing from above a British fighter squadron in its regulation V or line astern close formation. It translates as "the row of idiots".

Jagdbomber (Jabos)

This term referred to any of the *Luftwaffe* fighters that operated as fighter-bombers during the Battle of Britain, irrespective of whether these were *Messerschmitt Bf 109s* or *Bf 110s.*

Jagdfliegerführer (Jafu)

This post was created in both *Luftflotten* 2 and 3 as the assault began against Britain towards the end of July 1940. Theo Oesterkamp became *Jafu 2*, based in the Calais area and further west, the role of *Jafu 3* fell to Werner Junck. As the need to minimise the fuel problems of the Bf 109 increased, the latter's importance declined with most of these aircraft falling under the control of *Jafu 2.*

Jagdgeschwader (JG)

Luftwaffe fighter group of single engine aircraft.

Jagdwaffe

His was the generic term for the fighter component of the *Luftwaffe*.

Kampfgeschwader (KG)

Luftwaffe bomber group.

Kampfggruppe

Luftwaffe bomber wing.

Kanalkampf

The initial phase of the Battle of Britain where the main German air attacks were directed against Channel convoys and coastal facilities on the south coast.

Kanalkampfführer (Kanakafu)

Head of Channel Operations at the start of the *Luftwaffe* offensive against England.

Kanalkrankheit

Common term used by German aircrew to describe their anxiety of flying over the English Channel. It became common for many German airmen to need a desperate visit to the squadron latrines after mission briefings for this reason.

Lehrgeschwader (LG)

These were operational training groups within the *Luftwaffe*, deployed in 1940 to develop various tactical techniques. LG 2 operated two *Gruppen* equipped with Bf 109s, the first, *Jagd* (fighter), unit operating normally as conventional fighters and the second, *Schlacht* (ground attack), as *Jabos*.

Leutnant (Lt)

This was broadly equivalent to Pilot Officer in the RAF.

Luftflotten 2,3 and 5

The *Luftwaffe* was divided into independent (*Luftflotten*) Air Fleets on a geographical basis, each operating its own fleet of aircraft covering the full range of operations within the *Luftwaffe*, i.e. fighters, bombers, transports, reconnaissance or rescue aircraft. *Luftflotte 2* was based in Brussels during the summer of 1940 and had the main task of attacking southeast England and the London area. *Luftflotte 3* was based in Paris with their main target focus being the south and southwest of England and the industrial Midlands. *Luftflotte 5* was based in Stavanger in Norway and apart from a brief foray against the northeast of England in mid August 1940, limited their operational focus to defending the coast from Germany to Norway, as well as conducting shipping strikes in the North Sea.

Luftwaffe

The German Air Force.

Major

This was broadly equivalent to a Squadron Leader in the RAF.

Obergefreiter (Obgefr)

This was broadly equivalent to a Leading Aircraftsman in the RAF.

Oberkommando des Heeres (OKH)

German Army High Command.

Oberkommado der Luftwaffe (OKL)
Luftwaffe High Command.

Oberkommando der Wehrmacht (OKW)
Overall High Command for the German armed forces.

Oberleutnant (Oblt)
This was broadly equivalent to the rank of Flying Officer in the RAF.

Oberst
This was broadly equivalent to the RAF rank of Group Captain.

Reichsmarschall
On the 19th of July 1940, Hitler appointed Hermann Göring as his second in command, creating for him the new rank of Marshall of the German Reich and marking the occasion by handing Göring an elaborately crafted baton, signifying his elevated position of power. It speaks volumes for the closeness between Göring and Hitler at that time, in that Hitler felt it necessary to make a special gesture to his trusted ally from the start of the rise of National Socialism in Germany since the early 1930s. This was to some degree the result of the promotion of both Kesselring and Sperrle to the rank of *Generalfeldmarschall*, in recognition of their contribution to the victories that had been achieved since September 1939.

Rotte(n)
The basic formation for German fighter pilots, comprising two aircraft with the leader protected by his wingman throughout a sortie.

Schlageter
JG 26 adopted the unit name of *Schlageter* in honour of Albert Leo Schlageter who was executed in 1923 after a resistance mission against French occupying troops in Germany after World War One. With the rise of National Socialism in Germany in 1933, he became a hero of the Nazi party. JG 26's unit emblem adopted in his honour was a black gothic script letter "S" on a white shield.

Schwarm
Two pairs of German fighters operating in a loose, finger-four formation.

Seelöwe (Sea Lion)
Code name for the German invasion of southern Britain.

Seenotflug Kommando
These were the *Luftwaffe's* air-sea rescue units using mainly *Heinkel 59* seaplanes which were white-painted biplanes showing the red cross.

Stab

The headquarters' flight of either a *Geschwader* or a *Gruppe*, usually made up of 3 – 4 aircraft operated by the Commander of the unit, the Adjutant, the Technical Officer and occasionally another staff rank officer.

Staffel(n)

This was roughly equivalent in aircraft numbers to a squadron in the RAF. The *staffel* number was always shown as an Arabic number.

Staffelkapitän

This was the rank given to the leader of a *staffel*, which was broadly equivalent to the rank of Squadron Leader in the RAF in terms of the numbers of aircraft he controlled in action. Frequently in the Battle of Britain, the titular rank of the commanders of each level of unit could be more or less senior than this may suggest for operational reasons. In the early part of the conflict, his aircraft would be identified with the number "1", as well as carrying a small triangular pennant attached to the radio antenna aft of the cockpit.

Stuka

This was the commonly used name for the *Junkers* Ju 87 dive-bomber, actually an abbreviation of *Sturzkampflugzeug*, or dive-bomber. It gained a terrifying reputation among both civilians and the military on the ground from the Spanish Civil War until the summer of 1940. Used as aerial artillery in the support of an advancing ground offensive with limited opposing aircraft, it was an effective tool in the German arsenal. It was more vulnerable and generally less effective against Britain, which represented a fixed defensive position with a well-organised control network and modern, agile fighters.

Unteroffizier (Uffz)

This was broadly equivalent to Sergeant in the RAF.

Werke Nummer (W. Nr.)

German aircraft manufacturers assigned production numbers to completed aircraft for reference and spare parts reasons.

Zerstörer

This was the name by which the *Messerschmitt Bf 110* twin engine heavy fighter was generally known. Goering saw the units equipped with this aircraft as his elite units, able to provide fighter escort to bomber sorties deep into enemy territory. The aircraft had many positive features, but in close combat with agile single engine fighters it was revealed to be too cumbersome to turn and unable to accelerate quickly enough to survive. Some versions equipped for dive-bombing during the Battle of Britain were also delivered from the factories with the name *Jaguar* emblazoned on the fuselage nose.

Zerstörergeschwader (ZG)

This was a fighter wing equipped with twin engine (Bf 110) fighters.

A word from the author

A chance encounter at Duxford with one of the few surviving Messerschmitt Bf 109s from 1940 reignited a long dormant fascination with that part of World War 2. This restored aircraft came down some 1,000 metres from my present house and I couldn't resist the challenge to discover more about the local events of that time.

Since then, I have come to recognise how busy the skies were outside Sussex. This was particularly evident throughout the Channel coastal areas, where achieving air supeiority was the prerequisite for any practical invasion plans in the minds of German High Command. Kent, and particularly the coast around Dover, often referred to as "Hellfire Corner", can perhaps lay claim to being the most fertile of these areas in this respect, being the closest part of Britain that could be easily penetrated by the Luftwaffe fighter units after the evacuation of Dunkirk in June 1940.

Throughout the summer of 1940, the Kent countryside witnessed an enormous series of battles in the skies overhead. It began with the Channel attacks of July and early August, through the punishing German sorties against the south's airfields, the intensive daylight bombing of London that followed, and the last gasp of the *Luftwaffe* efforts against southern England using fighter-bombers as 1940 drew to a close.

I've read a number of books describing various aspects of life in Kent during the summer of 1940, as well as several well-researched works dealing with the airfields and units operating throughout the county at that time. These suggested that there is currently a gap in the coverage of the events in southeast England that I've done my best to identify and fill.

I set my sights on putting together a credible and readable account of the daily air battles that caused so many German and British casualties to litter the fields of Kent and the waters that surround the Garden of England. In doing this, it soon became clear that, despite a wealth of available information and literature covering this period, many accounts were contradictory in one area or another. The passage of time has also complicated this since the majority of the participants are no longer in a position to clarify what actually happened.

However, in order to present as complete a picture as possible while maintaining the closest possible link with facts, a degree of interpretation of events has been necessary. One example of this emerged when I constructed a detailed daily matrix identifying the known British and German casualties that resulted from the aerial battles that went on over Kent. Based on the geographical spread of these together with their recorded times, it became possible to link together the various opposing units that were involved in specific actions. This is in no way foolproof and I apologise to my readers for any glaring errors that may become apparent.

In addition to the aircraft that fell on land, most of which are well documented, I've tried to clarify in the daily picture of what happened *Luftwaffe* casualties that fell either in the waters around Kent or back in Europe. Most of these reports fail to identify the time of day they occurred, so I've tried to establish sensible links for these through the units involved for each mission. This could be viewed as tenuous but I've tried to use sensible criteria to achieve the result that is behind the narrative of the pages that follow.

Due to the volume of casualties over Kent throughout the summer of 1940, it's become necessary to split the continuous narrative into three volumes. The periods covered by each volume don't religiously follow the accepted definition of the different phases that are generally accepted for the Battle of Britain period. The length of each volume is dictated more by what seems to be a sensible length for each volume.

Volume one covers the build-up to the Battle of Britain following the evacuation from Dunkirk and continues through the Channel convoy attacks, the start of *Adlertag* and concludes during the last days of August when German airfield attacks were beginning to cause so much anxiety within the upper echelons of the RAF. Volume two follows the heavy damage and casualties incurred during the airfield attacks during the end of August and the first week of September, together with the start of the daylight raids on London. It concludes with the final major daytime assault on the capital in the middle of September. Volume three charts the final throes of the daylight bombing campaign against London during the last half of September and the subsequent fighter-bomber attacks that replaced them in daytime as the *Luftwaffe* bombers concentrated on the night offensive that continued until the spring of 1941. The narrative concludes as October 1940 draws to a close.

I don't believe I have a wholly-accurate appreciation of the events of this tumultuous period, but I hope the reader finds the picture portrayed both intriguing and engaging. Undoubtedly, some of my assumptions may be justifiably challenged but these have been made with the best of intentions in the hope that the narrative presents a credible and hopefully factual tribute to the bravery of the individuals who daily took to the skies over Kent, often perishing in the process.

East Dean – February 2015

May - June
Prelude

The Kent coastline around Dover and Folkestone has always represented an evocative sight for travellers arriving in Britain from the continent or more distant parts of the world. For most British people, it remains the symbol of a unique home which, for all its failings, is a special place, in some ways remote from the turmoil that may affect many other parts of the globe. In modern times, with international travel such an easy option by air, sea or rail, it's easy to forget what a barrier the Channel had been to all sorts of endeavours from the time when the British Isles physically split from the rest of continental Europe several hundred thousand years ago until the second half of the twentieth century. It's largely thanks to the Channel - just over twenty miles of water at its narrowest point - which separates Britain from France that most invasion plans against Britain have been doomed to failure since 1066.

Despite this, it's not surprising that from the mid-1930s the population of Kent and in particular those in the coastal towns around Dover began to feel decidedly apprehensive as the military expansion in Germany raised the spectre of new invasion threats from the continent, even before Britain declared war at the beginning of September 1939.

With the mobilisation of the British Expeditionary Force to join the French military in their joint campaign against Germany after the invasion of Poland, the ports of Dover, Folkestone, Ramsgate and the Medway towns became the gateway for military supplies and personnel to France. It was a ferry operator's dream, with military personnel and supplies going to France and returning holiday makers and British residents from overseas keeping the boats well occupied.

From the mid-1930s until war was declared, the coastal strip around Dover and other parts of the Kent coast saw a progressive defensive military build-up that would eventually see the bulk of the south coast beaches off-limits to the general population and covered with anti-invasion obstacles, artillery, anti-aircraft emplacements, a chain of powerful searchlights and other military facilities. Despite the confusing government evacuation programmes to and from London and other more remote parts of the country, the south coast saw a rash of commercial and private moves away from the coast, leaving many towns largely populated by the military, which in one form or another took over the majority of the seaside hotels, private houses, boarding houses and schools which had been vacated for the duration.

Dover became the focal point for many of these changes as the natural port of embarkation for France since it offered the shortest crossing. Just before the declaration of war, the harbour was dredged to offer maximum flexibility for the naval vessels that would be based there. New buoys were installed and it soon became clear that the harbour would become an important part of naval dispositions in the eastern end of the Channel. For an island economy with limited raw materials and food production, protection of shipping around Britain and particularly through the Channel and the Thames Estuary was a high priority.

As the prospect of war with Germany looked increasingly likely, many small civilian airfields throughout Kent were taken over by the military and most were subject to various expansion plans. By 1939, the Air Ministry was given the power to requisition surrounding tracts of land under the Emergency Powers (Defence) Act to allow these airfields to be brought up to RAF requirements. In many case these powers were used, much to the disgruntlement of the landowners involved, and by the autumn of 1939 Biggin Hill, Manston, Hawkinge and Gravesend were fully operational fighter airfields. The airfield at Lympne was also ready but classed as an emergency airfield, while those at Detling and Eastchurch came under Coastal Command rather than Fighter Command, even though they were occasionally used by fighter squadrons for one reason or another. During the late summer and autumn of 1940, various squadrons used the West Malling airfield as a temporary base or forward airfield, even though it became a more important fighter base later in the war.

Despite all the military preparations and disposition of British forces in both France and along the Belgian border, the eventual German assault in the west in May 1940 fulfilled Hitler's ambitions. It caught the Allied forces completely flat-footed with the surprise assault by armoured forces through the "impassable" Ardennes in a rapid thrust to the Channel coast around Boulogne.

The remnants of some of the BEF rescued from France return to the Channel ports after Operation Dynamo. Most escaped with limited equipment as can be seen from this picture where few have managed to retain even their Lee-Enfield rifles.

After the British retreat from Dunkirk that followed, the German forces in France concentrated on hastening the surrender of the remaining French units which continued to fight until the middle of June, culminating in the demeaning armistice signing on the 22nd of June at Compiègne. Hitler took great pleasure in holding the ceremony to sign the surrender document in the same railway carriage that the Allies had used to accept

Germany's surrender at the end of the Great War in 1918. Before the end of the "negotiations", he ordered the nearby monument to the 1918 Armistice to be blown up and then left in the early hours of the 23rd of June to begin a short sightseeing trip to Paris, which had effectively been declared an open city. Late at night the same day, he returned to *Wolf's Ravine*, his *Fall Röt* (the code name for the western offensive) headquarters at Brûly-de-Pesche, some 10 km from Bastogne in Belgium.

Hitler during his brief sightseeing visit to Paris on the 23rd of June 1940.

At the same time, many in the British government, the armed forces and the general public in Britain were anxiously anticipating some immediate follow-up to the German successes in France and the Low Countries in the form of the invasion of Britain. At the very least, it seemed reasonable to expect some form of attack in force on the demoralised and poorly-equipped British army in southern Britain – possibly an airborne assault on the Home Counties. Certainly, there were those among the German High Command that saw this as the most logical way to follow up the successes in Continental Europe and put an end to resistance throughout the west.

Time was, as always, a critical element. Even with the financial and raw material benefits of recent victories, the German economy simply wasn't prepared for a drawn-out conflict. Despite this, Hitler remained patient, convinced as he was that Britain must seek peace terms, having been so clearly defeated in France and the Low Countries. He spent some time visiting the old World War One battlefields he recalled from his own time fighting on the western front, as well as detouring to Dunkirk to take stock of the vast amount of military equipment abandoned by the retreating British Army. For weeks after the evacuation from Dunkirk, the German forces that moved into the Calais

– Dunkirk area were able to use the masses of abandoned tanks, guns and vehicles to supplement their own shortages.

Hitler was clearly conscious that Britain would have to be dealt with one way or another. However, even at this early stage, he was more concerned to find a way to deal with Russia whose defeat would give him access to the mineral and oil wealth that this vast country had to offer, at a stroke solving Germany's biggest strategic problem – lack of domestic raw materials.

Having just experienced outstanding success in the western campaign, a land war in which he felt qualified having served as a soldier during World War One, he was less comfortable with the idea of invading Britain. That would involve a campaign combining air and sea operations across the Channel as a necessary precursor to unleashing his *Blitzkrieg* land forces to steam-roller over southern Britain. He would not have wanted the adulation of the German population that followed the conquest of the Low Countries and France to be tarnished by the failure of a potentially vulnerable sea crossing to Britain, however ill-equipped the British army was after Dunkirk. The Royal Navy and the RAF still represented huge complications in such a venture.

On the 3rd of July, the British government demonstrated both to Hitler and the outside world that it had little intention of giving up the fight against Germany. With a view to denying Germany the use of the powerful French Navy at anchor in the harbour of Mers-el-Kébir in North Africa and other French bases away from mainland France, the Royal Navy delivered an ultimatum to the French naval commanders to sail their ships to various alternative locations in order to keep them from falling into the hands of the German *Kriegsmarine*, which possessed relatively few capital ships. With some unnecessary confusion over the terms presented to them, compounded it seems by some understandable reluctance on the part of the local French commanders, the time allowed for the French reply expired and the British fleet outside Mers-el-Kébir opened fire and caused many casualties and much damage to a number of the French ships. It remained an episode of the war that soured Anglo-French relationships for years to come.

After a triumphant victory parade through the streets of Berlin, acknowledging the adulation of the crowds, Hitler left Berlin on the 10th of July in search of the peace and solitude of his favourite home, the *Berghof*, high in the Bavarian mountains near Berchtesgarten. There, he could spend time mulling over the most sensible strategy against Britain and consulting with the heads of the different branches of the military that would be involved in any action necessary to subdue Britain. Throughout all this period, the potential threat of Russia and the material benefits of a successful campaign in the east probably hindered his ability to concentrate on the British problem.

It must have been a confusing time for Hitler, with his advisers suggesting courses of action that were often at odds with each other, as each of the branches of the armed forces sought to direct the course of any invasion plans to suit their own interests, simultaneously courting Hitler's favour. The *Führer* couldn't understand why the British government still hadn't put out peace feelers and he clung to the hope that time and diplomacy might achieve the risk-free solution that military action would only delay at a potentially-embarrassing cost.

The army wanted to mount a series of attacks across a wide front along the British south coast, seeing little difference, with the exception of distance, between an invasion across the English Channel and the numerous successful river crossings that had been involved in many of the campaigns since the previous autumn. The *Kriegsmarine*, under *Admiral* Raeder, knew the English Channel presented a whole host of complex problems that could lead to disaster if not dealt with in the right way. The Channel was, unlike most rivers, fraught with tidal problems, adverse currents, and a multitude of sand banks that precluded many direct approaches, as well as the threat from a still potent and nearby Royal Navy, not forgetting the RAF. The army also required a dawn landing which in itself meant a night crossing, potentially more risky, as well as also narrowing even further the potential range of windows where weather, timing and tidal conditions produced the ideal combination.

In all this, the one element that Hitler and both his army and naval advisers could at least agree on was that air superiority over the English Channel and southern Britain was essential. In order for a successful invasion of Britain to be carried out, Göring's *Luftwaffe* had to take control of the skies over the Channel and the Home Counties in the same way that they had over Poland, Scandinavia and the Low Countries.

While remaining aloof from most of the discussions that went on around the invasion plans, Göring was anxious to make up for the failure of his *Luftwaffe* to destroy the retreating British army on the beaches of Dunkirk. He desperately wanted the opportunity to launch mass air attacks on Britain and so force the British government to seek terms. He remained almost childishly anxious to court Hitler's favour, but frequently admitted to his own staff that he did not expect much to come of the plans to invade Britain. During the later joint service meetings that eventually forged what might have been a workable invasion plan, Göring chose not to attend, sending instead his Chief of Staff, *Generalmajor* Hans Jeschonnek.

By the 30th of June, Göring and his staff had already prepared plans for *Luftwaffe* operations across the Channel against Britain. One of the first steps taken was to send *Generalmajor* Kurt von Döring to the Calais area to set up a headquarters on the cliffs near Wissant, with its view across the 20 miles or so of water to Dover in Kent. One of von Döring's early tasks was to install one of the *Freya* radar sets on the cliffs to track convoy traffic through the Dover Straits, although this wasn't operational until towards the end of July.

German Intelligence remained curiously unaware of the significance of the tall radio masts that they could clearly see across the Channel near Dover. Nevertheless, they knew that Britain had some form of aerial radar detection, since they had captured mobile units that had been used by various air groups attached to the BEF in their efforts to repulse the German air fleets as they raided the Low Countries and France. Examination of the captured British equipment had convinced *General* Martini and his *Luftwaffe* communications group that their own technology was far in advance of the British equipment which they considered very rudimentary. This perhaps laid the groundwork for their continued inability to understand how well the permanent RDF system on the British coast did the job, irrespective of it being more basic. Basic or not, it worked most of the time and was fully integrated into the carefully-choreographed air detection and interception control system that had been devised and nurtured during the build-up to war in the late 1930s, primarily by Air Chief Marshall Hugh Dowding, the head of Fighter Command in the RAF. With the exception of radar itself, the fundamentals of the British air defence system had been established as a result of the problems encountered during World War One, and much of the communications structure required had already been put in place.

From the 2nd of July onwards, the *Luftwaffe* started to conduct raids across the Channel with small groups of bombers accompanied by fighter escorts on the lookout for British convoy traffic, the foremost target in this early part of the offensive against Britain. As the days passed, the raids would occasionally hit targets in mainland Britain, but the initial aim was to stifle the Channel shipping traffic and limit supplies for the British war effort. During this early part of the campaign against mainland Britain, Hitler had banned over-flying beyond the British coast, part of his plan to avoid what were seen as negative influences on any peace overtures that he expected to be forthcoming.

During the first few days of July, *Luftwaffe* forces conducted regular forays against the Channel convoy traffic. Fighter Command's commander, ACM Hugh Dowding, had resisted naval demands that the RAF should provide regular air cover for the convoys that hitherto had used the English Channel as the most expedient route to and from the Thames Estuary and London. The Royal Navy remained confident of its ability to forestall any air attacks that the *Luftwaffe* might make on convoy traffic until the 4th of July 1940 when an outbound Atlantic convoy (OA 178) came under heavy attack in the Portland area. The convoy of 35 merchant ships and two escorts had departed Southend on the 2nd of July, but was first attacked by a heavy force of Stuka dive-bombers from III / StG 51 off Portland around 0815 hours.. Most telling of all was the destruction of the auxiliary anti-aircraft ship, *Foylebank*, stationed in Portland harbour, which sank after sustaining some 22 bomb strikes. Several of the convoy's merchant vessels were sunk and many damaged during subsequent attacks by Stukas from I / StG 2and III / StG 51 (on their second mission of the day) as the convoy steamed westwards After this demonstration of the vulnerability to air attack of large groups of merchant and naval vessels in the Channel, the Admiralty routed all Atlantic convoys around the north of the British Isles. Local convoy traffic through the English Channel continued with Hugh Dowding having to accept that fighter patrols over the convoy routes during daylight hours were necessary, resulting in standing patrols of three to six aircraft generally operating in the vicinity of convoy traffic.

Across the channel from Kent in the Pas de Calais, *Luftflotte 2* was under the command of *Generalleutnant* Albert Kesserling, directing the overall disposition of the fighters and bombers in that area. Johannes Fink, the *Kommodore* of the bomber group KG 2, was appointed *Kanalkampfführer* (*Kanakafu* or Channel Battle Leader), in charge of the Air Fleet's operations in the area. He in turn appointed *Oberst* Theo Osterkamp, another veteran of World War One, to co-ordinate fighter operations in that part of the Channel area, whether this was related to escorting *Luftflotte 2* bombers or on fighter sweeps.

Initially, the principal fighter unit in the Calais area was JG 51 based at Guines, Marquise and St Omer, but JG 3 and JG 26 soon joined them in the area. The heavy fighter group *Zerstörergeschwader* (ZG) 26 (*Horst Wessel*) was also nominally attached to the region's fighter contingent.

It was during this early build-up to the Battle of Britain itself that the first casualties were suffered on both sides and Kent began to witness German aircraft force landing or crashing around the county. Initially these were a handful of Heinkel or Dornier bombers that had fallen foul of Spitfires and Hurricanes on either reconnaissance or bombing missions. These were mainly during daylight hours, but one Heinkel from the 6th *Staffel* / KG 4 had the misfortune to be shot down by a 19 Squadron Spitfire at 0215 hours on the morning of the 19th of June, ditching in the sea just off Sacketts Gap, near Margate.

The tail section of the KG 4 Heinkel He 111 shot down in the early hours of the 19th of June 1940. An unusual early morning casualty brought down by Fighter Command with the bomber's crew reaching shore and captivity in the aircraft's dinghy.

As the first week of July passed, the pace of Channel operations gradually increased. During these early encounters, with German sorties being mounted with numerous fighters loosely grouped together, Fighter Command's usual practice was to scramble a flight of three aircraft or a section of six machines to investigate. Hampered by their tight vic formations, where only the leader usually had a good view of the tactical situation they were faced with, these small formations were often bounced by superior numbers of unseen attackers while making their approach.

It was not until the 8th of July that Kent witnessed the first German fighter coming down intact in the British Isles. *Leutnant* Johann Böhm was flying with the 4th *Staffel* / JG 51 when his Bf 109 E-3, "White 4", was crippled during an attack by a Spitfire from 74 Squadron piloted by Sergeant Tony Mould. Hit in the fuel tank, the luckless *Jagdwaffe* pilot was unable to manoeuvre his faltering machine back to France and he made a force landing at Bladbean Hill, Elham around 1545 hours, so becoming the forerunner of what would eventually become a stream of German fighter pilots going into captivity over the next few months.

RAF personnel examine the first Messerschmitt Bf 109 to have landed virtually intact on British soil since the start if hostilities. The pilot, Leutnant Johann Böhm had been part of the 4th Staffel / JG 51.

Later the same evening, Flying Officer Desmond McMullen was leading a section of 54 Squadron Spitfires to intercept a formation of Bf 110s which had crossed the coast at Dungeness. As they were about to attack the Bf 110s, the Spitfires were themselves bounced by Bf 109s from above. Various claims were made by pilots from the 4th and 5th *Staffeln* / JG 51 for aircraft attacked around Dungeness and Dover, although it's impossible to connect the individual aircraft involved on each side of the fray. Two Spitfires from 54 Squadron were shot down and one damaged, but the only pilot casualty was Flying Officer Jack Coleman who was wounded and out of action for several weeks.

At 1930 hours, *Leutnant* Albert Striberny, of the 3rd *Staffel* (*Jagd*) / LG 2, was shot down by Coleman's colleagues in 54 Squadron. The German pilot baled out into captivity while his Bf 109 crashed near Sandwich in Kent. Striberny later recalled his last operation.

Having reached an altitude of 4,500m over the Channel we found ourselves in sunshine but saw that there were a lot of cumulus clouds over the English coast and Dover.... At about 1,700m, the clouds ended and together we flew over Dover.... I quickly noticed the Do 17 near us but then, much higher, saw the sun shining on many aircraft – Spitfires! Our situation was bad – low speed due to climbing through the cloud and so many aircraft coming down on us with the advantage of speed. I think now of the clear silhouette of our three aircraft against the white clouds.

In spite of our efforts to try and gain more speed, in no time they were on us and the battle was short. Whilst I was behind a Spitfire, another was behind me. I hear the sound as if one throws peas against a metal sheet and my cabin was full of dark smoke. I felt splashes of fuel on my face so I switched off the electrical system, dived back into the cloud and threw off the cabin roof. The smoke disappeared and I could breathe freely and noticed that from the wings there came white streams of glycol. Whilst diving, I tried several times to start the engine, switching on the electrical system, but in vain. When I came out of cloud, I decided to bail out and undid the clasp of my seat belt and was about to climb onto the seat and jump when I thought of the high speed of the aircraft and I was afraid to be thrown against the tailplane so I pulled back the stick and slow the aircraft down. This took a matter of seconds; I did a half roll and fell out.

The following day saw 54 Squadron in action several times. On the fourth sortie of the day from their forward base at Manston, "B" Flight Spitfires were involved in an operation that caused controversy on both sides. New Zealand Flight Lieutenant Al Deere was leading two sections of Spitfires to investigate unidentified contacts five miles east of Deal. After crossing the coast at 1,500 feet, Deere soon spotted what turned out to be a Heinkel He 59 float plane just above sea level, escorted by about 12 Bf 109s.

Detailing Yellow Section leader, Pilot Officer Johnny Allen, to attack the seaplane, Deere led Red Section to engage the German fighters. Allen succeeded in hitting the seaplane's engines which forced the aircraft to ditch over the Goodwin Sands, later being towed to Deal by the Walmer lifeboat, understandably becoming the subject of numerous photographs.

This type of seaplane was used by the German *Seenotflugkommando* to search the Channel for downed pilots, principally German fliers, but it wasn't unknown for British pilots to be rescued if found. In the eyes of the German fliers, the British attack on such an aircraft, clearly marked as a rescue craft with prominent red crosses, was barbaric and contrary to civilised rules of war. The seaplane's escorting Bf 109s reacted with understandable savagery to the attack on the seaplane.

As Allen attacked and forced down the He 59, Deere and his flight attacked the escorts, managing to damage one, but then the New Zealander found himself head-on with another Bf 109. Both pilots opened fire and within seconds they'd fleetingly collided, with the German aircraft passing over the top of Deere's cockpit, bending his propeller back horizontal and damaging his rudder. With his aircraft on fire, minimal control and with his engine stopped, Deere managed to glide back to land not far from Manston, suffering nothing apart from bruises, both physically and perhaps to his confidence.

The Heinkel He 59 B-2 from Seenotflug Kommando 1 shot down over the Goodwin Sands on the 9th of July 1940 which caused such controversy among Luftwaffe pilots. It was later beached near the Walmer Lifeboat Station in Kent.

The incident with the seaplane prompted protests from Germany, but the British Air Ministry issued a communiqué some three weeks later clarifying that bona fide rescue aircraft were free to pursue their rescue efforts provided they were operating solely for those purposes. However, where such aircraft were found in active areas of operation under escort from German fighters in such a way that they may be conducting reconnaissance operations, they would be considered a threat and dealt with accordingly. The incident continued to anger *Luftwaffe* personnel throughout the Battle of Britain and beyond.

By the 16th of July, Hitler had received the initial input from his subordinates in the various branches of the military and he gradually progressed towards the stage where an invasion of Britain could go ahead. Nevertheless, his uncertainty that this was the right course of action came across in the introductory wording to his *Führer* Directive No. 16 issued on the 16th of July.

> *Directive No. 16 - On preparations for a landing operation against England*
>
> *Since England, in spite of her hopeless military situation, shows no signs of being ready to come to an understanding, I have decided to prepare a landing operation against England and, if necessary, to carry it out.*

On the 19th of July, having returned to Berlin briefly from the *Berghof*, a massed rally was held at the *Kroll* Opera House in front of the *Reichstag*, where Hitler conferred decorations and promotion to *Feldmarschall* to 12 of the Generals that had led his victorious forces in the campaigns since September 1939, finally awarding the title of *Reichsmarschall* to Hermann Göring, the highest rank in the German armed forces. Hitler then launched into a speech of over two hours which many expected to contain some form of armistice proposal for Britain. It finished with what has come to be known as Hiltler's last appeal to reason.

> *In this hour I feel it to be my duty before my own conscience to appeal once more to reason and common sense, in Great Britain as much as elsewhere. I consider myself in a position to make this appeal since I am not the vanquished begging favours, but the victor speaking in the name of reason. I can see no reason why this war must go on.*
>
> *Possibly Mr Churchill will again brush aside this statement of mine by saying that it is merely of fear and doubt in our final victory. In that case, I shall have relieved my conscience in regards to the things to come.*

In order to bring this "peace" overture to as many in Britain as possible and despite the ban on operational sorties over mainland Britain, copies of the speech were air-dropped over many parts of Britain, on the assumption that if the general population of Britain realised Germany wanted to avoid further confrontation, they could make clear to the British government that negotiation with Germany was better than continued conflict.

Before leaving Berlin to indulge in a visit to the Wagner Festival being held in Bayreuth, Hitler met with his senior commanders at the Reich Chancellery. He made it clear to them that, unless Britain chose to open peace talks, he would authorise a combination of air and submarine attacks that would bring the British economy to such a low point that the invasion could go ahead in the middle of September as the coup-de-grâce.

Soon rebuffed both unofficially and officially, on the 21st of July, Hitler held the first joint services' meeting to hammer out the broad outline of a workable plan and timetable for the invasion of Britain. He lifted the ban on over-flying the British mainland on the 25th of July and issued *Führer* Directive No. 17 on the 1st of August 1940, the broad outline for the continued conduct of the war against Britain in its homeland.

Directive No. 17 - For the conduct of air and sea warfare against England

In order to establish the necessary conditions for the final conquest of England I intend to intensify air and sea warfare against the English homeland. I therefore order as follows:
1. The German Air Force is to overpower the English Air Force with all the forces at its command, in the shortest possible time. The attacks are to be directed primarily against flying units, their ground installations, and their supply organisations, but also against the aircraft industry, including that manufacturing anti-aircraft equipment.
2. After achieving temporary or local air superiority the air war is to be continued against ports, in particular against stores of food, and also against stores of provisions in the interior of the country.
Attacks on south coast ports will be made on the smallest possible scale, in view of our own forthcoming operations.
3. On the other hand, air attacks on enemy warships and merchant ships may be reduced except where some particularly favourable target happens to present itself, where such attacks would lend additional effectiveness to those mentioned in paragraph 2, or where such attacks are necessary for the training of air crews for further operations.
4. The intensified air warfare will be carried out in such a way that the Air Force can at any time be called upon to give adequate support to naval operations against suitable targets. It must also be ready to take part in full force in 'Operation Sea Lion'.
5. I reserve to myself the right to decide on terror attacks as measures of reprisal.
6. The intensification of the air war may begin on or after 5th August. The exact time is to be decided by the Air Force after the completion of preparations and in the light of the weather.
The Navy is authorised to begin the proposed intensified naval war at the same time.

July – Kanalkampf
The Channel Battles

10th July 1940

While the weather over most of the country suffered from fairly continuous rain, it was showery over southeast England and the Channel, allowing limited air operations in the area.

Using the marginal weather conditions for concealment, a Dornier Do 17 P was sent on reconnaissance over the Channel at around 1030 hours, escorted by the whole of I / JG 51. Six Spitfires from 74 Squadron were scrambled from Hornchurch, intercepting the Dornier and its escorts some 30 minutes later. The Dornier was damaged during the British fighters' attacks, as were three Spitfires from 74 Squadron which all force landed at forward airfields on the south coast.

As the damaged Dornier and its escorts returned to France, another *Staffel* of Bf 109s patrolled the south coast on the lookout for any tempting targets. Obligingly, Spitfires from 610 Squadron at Biggin Hill were vectored towards them, and another melée ensued, after which the leader of the British formation was obliged to force land his machine at Hawkinge.

This was the ominous forerunner for the pattern of operations during the rest of the day. Off North Foreland, the reconnaissance Dornier had spotted a large convoy, CW3 (codenamed *Bread*), heading in ballast towards the Dover Straits and had radioed the sighting in to *Luftflotte 2*. Armed with this intelligence, Johannes Fink, the *Kommodore* of KG 2, put together a force of 24 Dornier Do 17s from his own I / KG 2, escorted by 30 Messerschmitt Bf 110s from ZG 26 and 20 Messerschmitt Bf 109s from JG 51.

When convoys were transiting the Dover Straits, Fighter Command's Commander-in-Chief, Hugh Dowding, was reluctantly obliged to maintain standing patrols over the convoy traffic. In the case of CW3, this consisted of a flight of six Hurricanes from 32 Squadron which had been scrambled from Biggin Hill at 1315 hours. However, as soon as the size of the *Luftwaffe* force became clear, these were supplemented by further aircraft scrambled some 15 minutes later. These included 56 Squadron from North Weald which was using Manston as its forward base, together with elements of 64 Squadron from Kenley, 74 Squadron from Hornchurch and 111 Squadron from Croydon. What followed was the largest dogfight seen so far over the Channel and this has generally become viewed as the starting point of the Battle of Britain.

The skies off the Folkestone coast bore witness to fierce fighting as the pilots from both sides fought and jockeyed for position. On this occasion, the RAF came out of the action arguably better than the *Luftwaffe*. While four Hurricanes returned to base or forward airfields with battle damage, only one was lost when it collided with one of the German bombers as 111 Squadron made a head-on attack that broke up the German bomber formation. The British pilot, Flying Officer Tom Higgs, managed to bale out as his aircraft span towards the sea minus one of its wings, but he was killed and his body was washed ashore just over one month later on the Dutch coast.

On the *Luftwaffe* side however, the losses assumed far greater significance. While the only casualty of the early morning reconnaissance mission had been the damaged

Dornier which force landed on the French coast, the afternoon sortie had an altogether different outcome.

A Dornier Do 17 Z from KG 2 in formation typical of the aircraft sent to attack the Channel convoy on the 10th of July 1940.

Hauptmann Hannes Trautloft of III / JG 51 is said to have commented on the action over "Bread" by saying:

Suddenly the sky was full of British fighters. Today we were going to be in for a tough time.

As with most of these actions, there are differing accounts of the damage suffered. Within the escort formations, it seems clear that one Bf 109 from the 5th *Staffel* / JG 51 was lost and two more from the 7th *Staffel* were damaged and force landed in France without serious injury to the pilots. *Oberfeldwebel* Artur Dau of the 7th *Staffel* was the pilot of one of the damaged machines and he later recalled:

The whole cockpit stank of burnt insulation but I managed to stretch my glide to the coast and made a belly landing close to Cherbourg. As I jumped out, the machine was on fire and within seconds, ammunition and fuel went up with a bang.

It's possible that Dau's Bf 109 was the same one described in the combat report of Pilot Officer Peter St John of 74 Squadron.

I was No. 3 in Yellow section patrolling over a convoy off Deal at about 10,000 ft. C.B.1200 visibility good. I sighted three enemy aircraft below and to the right. I informed Yellow leader of them; we went into line astern and went down to engage enemy aircraft. On the way down I saw another formation of 109's to the left and slightly down. Yellow leader had seen them also and we climbed and attacked from the rear. The 109's split up and I picked one and gave him a short deflection burst. I did not have time to see the effect of the burst as another 109 was on my tail. I outclimbed the 109 without difficulty. When I got on his tail I gave him all the ammunition I had and saw my tracers going in. The 109 flew off very unsteadily towards the French coast. Having finished all my ammunition I returned to Base. In my estimation there were about thirty 109's. I did not see any bombs.

Artur Dau continued flying on operations across the Channel until the end of August when he was shot down over Kent, baling out to become a POW.

The Bf 110s from ZG 26 did not fare so well, ominously demonstrating that these heavy machines required intelligent deployment in order to use their speed, high altitude capability and firepower to the best advantage. On the 10th July, they flew not far above the KG 2 bombers and suffered numerous casualties as the more nimble British fighters attacked the bombers and their close escorts. On this occasion, three Bf 110s from the 8th *Staffel* / ZG 26 were shot down with the loss of all crew members, only one of whom was taken prisoner of war. Two further machines were damaged but returned to France, one minus the *Bordfunker* (radio operator/gunner), who'd apparently baled out over the Channel.

Despite these losses, the *Jagdwaffe* units had been unable to prevent the bombers from being attacked in their approach to bomb the rapidly-manoeuvring convoy. Arguably, it had been the head-on attack made by the Hurricanes of 111 Squadron that upset the ordered procession of the Dorniers.

The convoy had been sighted between Dover and Dungeness. Our briefing took only a few minutes and within half an hour of being airborne, we sighted the coast of Kent. The Channel was bathed in brilliant sunshine. A light haze hung over the English coast, and there, far below us, was the convoy, like so many toy ships with wispy white wakes fanning out behind. As soon as we were observed, the ships of the convoy dispersed, the merchantmen manoeuvring violently and the escorting warships moving out at full speed. Anti-aircraft shell peppered the sky. Our fighters now appeared. We made our first bomb run, and fountains leapt up around the ships. By now the fighter squadrons of the Royal Air Force had joined in, and the sky was a twisting, turning melée of fighters. My wing was in the air for three hours in all. We reported one heavy cruiser and four merchant ships sunk, one merchant ship damaged, and eleven British fighters shot down or damaged. We had lost two bombers, two twin engine fighters and three single engine fighters during the course of this engagement.

Located in Kent at Swingate near Dover, this structure is typical of the three Chain Home transmitter masts that formed part of facilities that allowed aircraft approaching the coast to be located and tracked.

All German medium bombers had been designed with the crew enclosed close together in clear plexiglass nose compartments, mostly with armour plating located to protect the crew from attacks from the rear. For these airmen, the sight of a fighter squadron approaching from the front at a closing speed of something like 500 mph with guns blazing would have been a frightening and unsettling sight. In this case, the *Staffelkapitän* of the 3rd *Staffel* / KG 2, *Hauptmann* Walter Krieger, had the misfortune to collide with Tom Higgs' attacking Hurricane, crashing into the sea at 1400 hours near the Dungeness Buoy. Some reports suggested that Krieger's Dornier had been the victim of AA fire from the convoy's escorts. He was captured along with one of his crew, the other two NCOs being recorded as missing.

For the remainder of the bomber formation, surrounded by zooming Messerschmitts, Spitfires and Hurricanes, this must have been a salutary spectacle. Whether the cause was an intended ramming or, more likely, collision due to high closing speed, the visual impact would have been profoundly unsettling for the remaining bomber crews.

Three further Dorniers returned to France damaged in the action, one seriously, the unit suffering a total of four crew members killed and six wounded. Another machine had been shot down into the sea by a combination of attacks from the British fighters and AA fire. Yet another Dornier from II / KG 2 was lost during the day, but the circumstances of the loss are unclear and possibly unconnected with the convoy's attack. Of the ships in the convoy, only one small vessel was actually sunk.

11th – 12th July 1940

Over the next two days, the Channel area was affected by low cloud and some early morning fog, discouraging a resumption of the level of operations seen on the 10th of July. Despite this, attacks continued against convoy Bread as it steamed across Lyme Bay in the west and some raids were mounted against two other convoys, *Agent* off North Foreland and *Booty* on the east coast, off Orfordness. The bulk of the German attacks were against the latter convoy.

With RAF Fighter Command having shown its determination to protect the coastal convoy traffic, it had already become evident that JG 51 alone would have some problems covering any future bomber raids on shipping. Osterkamp's unit received additional support initially in the form of III / JG 3 under *Hauptmann* Walter Kienitz which moved into Guines near Calais. They were followed over the next few days by other fighter units, including JG 26 *Schlageter*.

13th July 1940

Persistent fog over southern England limited operations during the early morning although this gradually cleared by midday. Convoy activity continued in the Channel, attracting afternoon attacks by *Luftflotte 3* in the west around Portland and *Luftflotte 2* around Dover.

During the later afternoon, a small group of Ju 87 Stukas from II / *Stuka Geschwader* (StG) 1, escorted by Bf 109s from Theo Osterkamp's JG 51, attacked convoy CW4 (codenamed *Agent*) as it was passing south of Dover. The convoy had left Southend the previous day with some 18 merchant vessels, apparently unaccompanied by any escort vessels. Eleven Hurricanes from North Weald's 56 Squadron were vectored onto the German formation, later reinforced by Spitfires from Kenley's 64 Squadron.

JG 51 had been assigned the escort role, with some of the Bf 109s operating as close escort for the Stukas. The JG 51 *Geschwader Kommodore*, *Oberleutnant* Theo Osterkamp was leading the *Stab* (Headquarters) Flight, while the close escort fighters were under the command of one of the *Jagdwaffe's* rising stars, *Oberleutnant* Josef Fözö, who later remarked on the evening sortie.

> *Unfortunately for them (the Hurricanes), they slid into position between the Stukas and our close escort Messerschmitts. We opened fire and at once three Hurricanes separated from the formation, two dropping and one gliding down to the water smoking heavily. At that instant I saw a Stuka diving in an attempt to reach the French coast. It was chased by a single Hurricane. Behind the Hurricane was a 109, and behind that, a second Hurricane, all of the aircraft firing at the one in front. I saw the deadly dangerous situation and rushed down. There were five aircraft diving in a line towards the water.*

> *The Stuka was badly hit and both crewmen wounded; it crashed on the beach near Wissant. The leading Messerschmitt, flown by Feldwebel John, shot down the first Hurricane into the water, its right wing appeared above the waves like the dorsal fin of a shark before it sank. My Hurricane dropped like a stone close to the one that John had shot down.*

The unfortunate Hurricane pilots appear to have been Sergeants James Cowsill and Joe Whitfield who were both listed as missing during this evening sortie. Sergeant Cowsill was the pilot who'd caused the damage to the dive-bomber that had crash-landed on the coast near Wissant, but he'd been unable to avoid *Feldwebel* Hans John's attack.

The reports of the encounter from the surviving pilots of 56 Squadron showed the tendency towards over-claiming in the confusion of the hectic combat that followed this clash over the Channel off Dover. Several of the *Stukas* and a number of the fighter escorts were claimed as destroyed with others listed as damaged. In reality, only two of the German dive-bombers were damaged and towards the end of the engagement one of the Bf 109s piloted by *Leutnant* Lange was shot down. He was killed when his aircraft crashed in Holland, possibly the victim of Sub-Lieutenant Frank Paul, a Fleet Air Arm pilot seconded to fly Spitfires with 64 Squadron.

Belying his advanced years, Theo Osterkamp put in a claim for a Spitfire that he'd engaged during this sortie. His victim was another pilot from Kenley's 64 Squadron, Sergeant Arthur Binham, whose Spitfire was also hit by AA fire whilst in action off the

Dover coastline. Binham managed to bring his damaged aircraft for a force landing at Hawkinge and the pilot emerged unhurt.

Oberleutnant Theo Osterkamp, Geschwader Kommodore of JG 51, a veteran of the First World War, became Jagdfliegerführer 2, controlling all the fighters that became attached to Luflotte 2 in the Pas de Calais area.

14th July 1940

With fair weather during the day, the *Luftwaffe* continued its attacks on the Channel convoys, extending their growing dominance over this strategic waterway. Convoy CW3 (codenamed *Bread*) was attacked off Swanage in the west, while convoy CW5 (codenamed *Pilot*) left Southend, also bound for the West Country.

Three *Staffeln*, some 30 Ju 87 dive-bombers, from *Hauptmann* Bernd von Brauchitsh's IV (Stuka) / *Lehrgeschwader* (LG) 1 were dispatched to attack the convoy off Dover. The Stukas were escorted by Bf 109s from JG 3 which had previously been stationed further west in France after the British evacuation from Dunkirk and the fall of France.

Shortly after 1500 hours, the Stukas arrived over Dover and proceeded to bomb the convoy of ten vessels. These were protected by six Hurricanes from 615 Squadron's "A" Flight, but once the approaching German formation had been picked up by radar and the Observer Corps., they were joined by seven more Hurricanes from 151 Squadron based at Rochford in Essex. Further reinforcements arrived in the form of 12

Spitfires from 610 Squadron, together with 615 Squadron's "B" Flight which had been waiting at readiness at Hawkinge on the hills behind Folkestone.

The initial interception by the first Hurricanes took place around 1515 hours and 615 Squadron Hurricanes brought down one of the Ju 87 Stukas which crashed into the sea off Dover with the loss of its crew, *Oberleutnant* Sonnberg and his gunner. As the Bf 109s fought to protect the vulnerable dive-bombers and the German force withdrew back to France, they were pursued by the Spitfires of 610 Squadron which succeeded in damaging two of the Bf 109s. One of these was so badly damaged that its wounded pilot baled out before the aircraft crashed near Boulogne, and the second returned to Wissant with the pilot unhurt.

The action was not all one-sided, however. During the attacks, the Norwegian flag *Balder* (1,129 tons) was bombed and set on fire with four killed and 10 wounded, before being towed to Dover for repairs. The British flag *Island Queen* (779 tons) was sunk and the British flag *Mons* (641 tons) had her boiler burst and was also towed into Dover.

A pilot from IV Gruppe / LG 1 runs up the Jumo engine of his Junkers Ju 87 B during the early summer of 1940.

The whole engagement had been under the comparatively close scrutiny of a young BBC radio reporter, Charles Gardner, who had arrived earlier on the Dover cliffs overlooking the Straits, equipped with a recording van. During the afternoon, he was to witness and record his observations and reactions to the spectacle of the convoy under attack by the German formations from across the Channel, broadcasting his commentary to the nation. From today's perspective of instant communication and live video footage from around the world, it's perhaps difficult to appreciate how radical a development this was, and how shocking to some of the population such vivid accounts seemed.

When it was broadcast, it caused something of an uproar. Many people in Britain felt that such an eye-witness account was too dramatic, and entirely inappropriate for broadcasting as 'news', reducing a life-and-death struggle between combatants to the level of a sporting contest.

The Germans are dive-bombing a convoy out at sea; there are one, two, three, four, five, six, seven German dive-bombers, Junkers 87s. There's one going down on its target now — Bomb! No! He missed the ships, it hasn't hit a single ship — there are about ten ships in the convoy, but he hasn't hit a single one and — There, you can hear our anti-aircraft going at them now. There are one, two, three, four, five, six — there are about ten German machines dive-bombing the British convoy, which is just out to sea in the Channel.

I can't see anything. No! We thought he had got a German one at the top then, but now the British fighters are coming up. Here they come. The Germans are coming in an absolute steep dive, and you can see their bombs actually leave the machines and come into the water. You can hear our guns going like anything now. I am looking round now. I can hear machine gunfire, but I can't see our Spitfires. They must be somewhere there. Oh! Here's one coming down. There's one going down in flames. Somebody's hit a German and he's coming down with a long streak — coming down completely out of control — a long streak of smoke — and now a man's baled out by parachute. The pilot's baled out by parachute. He's a Junkers 87, and he's going slap into the sea — and there he goes. SMASH! A terrific column of water and there was a Junkers 87. Only one man got out by parachute, so presumably there was only a crew of one in it.

It's unclear whether the "Ju 87" that Charles Gardner described was *Oberleutnant* Sonnberg's aircraft or whether in fact it was Pilot Officer Michael Mudie's Hurricane that crashed into St Margaret's Bay during this engagement. If Charles Gardner actually saw the pilot baling out of the aircraft that he witnessed crashing into the sea, it was probably the Hurricane rather than the Stuka, since there are no records of either of the Stuka's crew being picked up. With no disrespect to Charles Gardner, aircraft identification at any distance is an art often fraught with the potential for misidentification even for the experienced, particularly when many different aircraft are operating in the same patch of sky, as the reporter's next comments revealed.

Now, then, oh, there's a terrific mix-up over the Channel!! It's impossible to tell which are our machines and which are Germans.

There was one definitely down in this battle and there's a fight going on. There's a fight going on, and you can hear the little rattles of machine gun bullets. Grump! That was a bomb, as you may imagine. Here comes one Spitfire. There's a little burst. There's another bomb dropping. Yes. It has dropped. It has missed the convoy. You know, they haven't hit the convoy in all this. The sky is absolutely patterned with bursts of anti-aircraft fire, and the sea is covered with smoke where the bombs have burst, but as far as I can see there is not one single ship hit, and there is definitely one German machine down. And I am looking across the sea now. I can see the little white dot of parachute as the German pilot is floating down towards the spot where his machine crashed with such a big fountain of water about two minutes ago.

The critically-injured Michael Mudie was eventually picked up from out of the sea by a Royal Navy vessel and hastily transferred to Dover Hospital for treatment. That same evening the BBC broadcast Charles Gardner's recording, an action which was later criticised in some quarters as having lacked dignity towards a life and death struggle.

Tragically, Michael Mudie succumbed to his wounds the following day. On Thursday 18th July Flying Officer Lionel Gaunce and Pilot Officer Cecil Montgomery travelled from RAF Kenley to East Molesey in Surrey, to represent 615 Squadron at the funeral of their fallen comrade, where he rests to this day in a well-kept grave, respectfully tended to ensure his sacrifice is not forgotten.

The BBC reporter continued his broadcast as the German formation withdrew to France under pressure for the British fighters that had been sent to protect the convoy.

Now — hark at the machine guns going! Hark! one, two, three, four, five, six; now there's something coming right down on the tail of another. Here they come; yes, they are being chased home — and how they are being chased home! There are three Spitfires chasing three Messerschmitts now. Oh, boy! Look at them going! Oh, look how the Messerschmitts! — Oh boy! that was really grand!

There's a Spitfire behind the first two. He will get them. Oh, yes. Oh, boy! I've never seen anything so good as this. The R.A.F. fighters have really got these boys taped. Our machine is catching up the Messerschmitt now. He's catching it up! He's got the legs of it, you know. Now right in the sights. Go on, George! You've got him! Bomb — bomb. No, no, the distance is a bit deceptive from here. You can't tell, but I think something definitely is going to happen to that first Messerschmitt. Oh yes — just a moment — I think I wouldn't like to be in that first Messerschmitt. I think he's got him. Yes? Machine guns are going like anything. No, there's another fight going on. No, they've chased him right out to sea. I can't see, but I think the odds would be certainly on that first Messerschmitt catching it

Oh, look! Where? Where? I can't see them at all. Just on the left of those black shots. See it? Oh, yes, oh yes, I see it. Yes, they've got him down, too. I can't see. Yes, he's pulled away from him. Yes, I think that first Messerschmitt has been crashed on the coast of France all right.

Believed to be one of a series of photos of a convoy off the Kent coast attacked by Stukas during July 1940. The naval escort on the right appears to be making smoke to provide cover for the convoy's vessels from the German attacks.

The damaged and smoking Messerschmitts that the reporter referred to were probably the two machines from JG 3's 8th *Staffel* that struggled back to France with one of the pilots wounded.

Charles Gardner's commentary on the day's engagement off Dover was not the only controversial issue of the 14th of July 1940. Air Ministry instructions were circulated to squadrons that they were to treat the *Seenotflugkommando* (air sea rescue unit) seaplanes as legitimate targets, irrespective of their markings. It was common practice for these aircraft to be painted white and carry both civilian registration and Red Cross markings. Air Chief Marshall Hugh Dowding, head of Fighter Command, took the wholly dispassionate but ruthless view that, while these aircraft were engaged in rescuing German and sometimes British airmen from the sea, they were generally recovering crew members who would be able to fly again in the German air assault on Britain. It was also his view that if such aircraft were granted immunity from attack for humanitarian reasons, their crews would be able to provide valuable reconnaissance intelligence as they pursued their recovery efforts.

15th – 18th July 1940

Monday the 15th of July saw low cloud covering much of the country, accompanied by occasional heavy rain. During the morning, *Luftwaffe* activity involved mostly reconnaissance missions. These revealed convoy CW 5 (codenamed *Pilot*) proceeding westwards towards Swanage and *Oberst* Johannes Fink sent 15 Do 17s from KG 2 to attack the convoy, reaching it at 1413 hours. They were hampered in their attack by Hurricanes from 56 and 151 Squadrons, but there were no recorded casualties from either side of this engagement.

The build-up of Bf 109 units on bases around the Pas de Calais gathered pace as I / JG 26 moved its aircraft into the area, occupying farmland at Audembert. The remaining *Gruppen* of JG 26 moved to nearby locations by the 21st of July.

During this early period of the Battle of Britain, JG 26 was under the command of *Major* Gotthard Handrick, who remained *Geschwader Kommodore* until Göring replaced him with one of the younger rising stars of the *Jagdwaffe*, *Major* Adolf Galland, then *Kommandeur* of III / JG 26. This fighter wing would remain stationed at bases in the Pas de Calais area long after the Battle of Britain was over, withdrawing only for brief periods of rest to bases further in the east. Ultimately, they would withdraw as the Allied invasion of Normandy in June 1944 made continued operations from north France impractical, but not before earning an enviable reputation as an effective fighter unit, particularly valued for its bomber escort tactics.

Fog covered North France, the Dover Straits and southeast England the following day, conditions that remained obstacles to air operations on any scale over Kent and the southeast. This situation remained problematic for the next few days, with the weather staying dull with occasional rain.

Despite the cloudy, cool, rainy weather around the Dover Straights, there were sporadic raids on the Channel ports and shipping in the area. Early during the morning of the 18th of July, one of the German patrols over the Channel was intercepted by the Spitfires from Biggin Hill's 610 Squadron off the Kent coast around Deal.

The only recorded casualty of that Thursday was Pilot Officer Peter Litchfield of 610 Squadron, whose Spitfire was shot down in the Channel at 0955 hours some 15 km north of Calais with the British pilot posted as missing. The British pilot was probably the victim of *Hauptmann* Horst Tietzen, *Staffelkapitän* of the 5th *Staffel* / JG 51. Litchfield had been one of the 610 Squadron pilots that had pursued the German formations back across the Channel four days earlier and it was he who was credited with the two Bf 109s that had been damaged on that day. His fate was typical of those that haunted Dowding and Park as they strove to keep their pilots within the relative safety of the skies over southern England itself, rather than the more threatening environment over the Channel and the north French coast.

As Litchfield's luck ran out on the 18th of July, he became the 8th claim made by the Condor Legion veteran "Jakob" Tietzen who went on to score 20 kills in the Battle of Britain before he was himself shot down into the waters of the Thames Estuary one month later.

19th July 1940

The weather continued showery with bright intervals, light winds and scattered cloud over the Channel. This would be a day of major calamity for the RAF in the southeast.

Decisions on aircraft procurement taken by the Air Ministry in the build-up to war during the late 1930s clearly demonstrated the dangers of assuming the strategic situation would remain as it was foreseen before the outbreak of hostilities between Germany and the rest of Europe. The frighteningly quick fall of the Low Countries and France allowed the German forces to adopt tactics that made some of the Air Ministry's earlier decisions appear decidedly ill-advised.

The Boulton-Paul Defiant heavy fighter armed with four Browning .303 inch machine guns in the electrically-powered rear turret designed mainly for attacks on unescorted bombers.

By early afternoon, the outcome of an engagement over Dover clearly showed that it was not just the Messerschmitt Bf 110 that lacked the qualities to hold its own with the new generation of nimble single-engine fighters from both sides.

The Boulton-Paul Defiant had been the result of Air Ministry specifications for a new interceptor to tackle unescorted bombers attacking directly from Germany. The possibility of German occupation of the north French coast had understandably not been factored into this decision, with the result that any squadrons operating the Defiant in daylight within the combat range of the Messerschmitt Bf 109s based around Calais were in grave danger once France fell to Germany.

The aircraft, similar in some ways to the appearance of the Hurricane that was issued to the majority of squadrons in Fighter Command, was equipped with a power-operated gun turret carrying four Browning machine guns that could be traversed to cover from one side to the other and to the rear. It soon became clear that the weight of this equipment was a fatal handicap when faced with the *Jagdwaffe's* Bf 109 fighters. The loaded weight of the Defiant was over 8,300 lb, compared with the Spitfire at 5,900 lb and the Hurricane at 6,600 lb, all three aircraft being powered by the same Rolls Royce Merlin engine, rated at 1,030 hp. This alone meant that the Defiant would take up to two minutes more to reach 20,000 feet compared to either of the two single seat fighters, a severe handicap when advance warning of impending raids was limited. By comparison, the Bf 109 E was a relative featherweight, with a loaded weight of just over 5,500 lb.

The fatal flaw in deciding to operate this aircraft as a day fighter within the operating radius of Bf 109s stationed in North France and the Low Countries was that this adverse weight differential also seriously limited the speed and manoeuvrability of the Defiant. This was not the only problem. An additional disadvantage was that the aircraft lacked any forward armament controlled by the pilot, the result being an aircraft which was difficult to co-ordinate in terms of the direction of flight and the control of the aircraft's gunfire in a dogfight.

The Defiants had enjoyed limited success in the French campaign where the aircraft's plan-view had initially been mistaken for the Hurricane, with German pilots attacking from the normally safe position astern of their target finding themselves facing the concentrated firepower of four Browning machine guns operated by the gunner. Nevertheless, the Defiant soon demonstrated its limitations in fighter versus fighter combat, being particularly vulnerable when attacked from below and to the rear, out of the effective radius of the turret's defensive fire. However, in the early days of the Battle of Britain, aircraft numbers were a critical concern until production of new machines had replaced the many aircraft lost during May and June 1940, so there were limited options to keep this comparatively modern machine away from the action in the southeast during daylight.

At noon on the 19th of July, Theo ("*Onkel*") Osterkamp led III / JG 51 from the unit's airfield outside St Omer to escort Bf 110 fighter-bombers from the 1st and 2nd Staffel of the recently-formed specialist precision bombing unit, *Erprobungsgruppe 210*. They were due to make an attack against an armed trawler in the area around Dover harbour. Some 18 minutes after take-off, the fighter-bombers dived to attack the zigzagging anti aircraft vessel, thereafter returning to their home base unmolested.

Since they had encountered no RAF reception committee, Osterkamp decided that he would use the fuel remaining after such a brief sortie to see if any British fighters had been scrambled to provide air cover for the ships in the Dover sector. With the fighter-bombers safely shepherded back over France, he led his formation back out over the Channel to see what might appear.

The Stabschwam of III / JG 51.Oberleutnant Otto Kath is on the left and Hauptmann Hannes Trautloft is on the right. (Via Goss)

Shortly after noon, nine Defiants from 141 Squadron, based at West Malling, took off from their advanced base at Hawkinge for their first patrol 20 miles south of Folkestone. As they climbed to patrol height in tight formation, they unwittingly flew below the fighters from JG 51. *Major* Hannes Trautloft's *Stabschwarm* (Headquarters flight) from III / JG 51 was flying at close to 10,000 feet, with the remainder of the *Jagdwaffe* group some 3,000 feet higher still. Due to the time of day, with the sun almost directly overhead, the German formation was not spotted until Trautloft's *schwarm* made a diving attack at 1243 hours. Immediately, the Defiants that could bring their guns to bear turned the full force of their combined firepower on the diving Bf 109s which had to withstand a tremendous barrage of machine gun fire. Trautloft later recalled:

Suddenly, all hell broke loose. The Englishmen had seen us. Defensive fire from a number of turrets flew towards me – fireworks all over the place. I could see the bullets passing by on either side and felt hits on my machine, but pressed home the attack. 200m, 100m – now was the time to fire and my machine guns and cannons hammered away. The first volley was too high but the second was right in the middle of the fuselage and parts of the Defiant broke loose and flashed past me. I saw a thin smoke trail appear below the fuselage and suddenly the aircraft exploded in a huge red ball of flames which fell towards the sea.

Trautloft's colleagues were not far behind and 141 Squadron was badly hit, with six aircraft destroyed and a further machine returning to base badly damaged. Of the 14 crew from these aircraft, only two survived, with one of these wounded. The remainder were either killed or posted as missing in the Channel, with the most vulnerable being the gunners who faced huge problems baling out. Two days later, 141 Squadron was moved north to Prestwick in Ayrshire, fortunately well beyond the range of the aircraft that had decimated the unit.

It was not all one-sided, despite the carnage suffered by 141 Squadron. Both Trautloft and the *Gruppe Adjutant, Oberleutnant* Otto Kath, had the unenviable task of nursing their damaged machines back across the Channel. Trautloft recalled the thoughts that must have crossed the minds of many young *Luftwaffe* pilots forced to deal with similar problems during the weeks that followed.

........And then suddenly my engine vibrated and began to run unevenly. I could smell burning oil in the cockpit and my coolant temperature indicated 120 degrees with the oil temperature also rising steadily. For the first time, I noticed several hits on my left wing and a trail of smoke beneath it. I felt uneasy – I didn't want to have to bale out in the middle of the Channel.

Then Kath appeared on my left. His aircraft was also trailing smoke. "I've got to make an emergency landing" he told me over the WT, and like me, headed towards the French coast.

It's a damned uneasy feeling flying so slowly over the sea in a shot-up crate, all the more worrying when one's flying height was diminishing steadily – and all the while, the coast didn't seem to be getting any closer. Luckily there weren't any enemy fighters around or we'd have been easy meat.

Both Trautloft and Kath scraped over the French coast, and managed to force land their aircraft nearby. A third aircraft from the 9th *Staffel* of JG 51, flown by *Feldwebel*

Heilmann, had been heavily damaged by the Defiants but also managed to return to base. The pilot sadly died of his wounds.

Later that afternoon, *Erprobungsgruppe 210* returned to the Dover area and made another attack on shipping. After refuelling and re-arming following the earlier sortie, they took off from St Omer, again escorted by JG 51, and sank the Admiralty oiler, *War Sepoy,* as well as damaging the destroyer *HMS Griffin*, a tug and a drifter, before withdrawing back to France without suffering any casualties. 11 Group sent fighters from 32, 64 and 74 squadrons to intercept the raid, and the Hurricanes and Spitfires from these units became embroiled in action with the Bf 109s from JG 51.

One of the Spitfires flown by Flying Officer Bert Woodward was involved in a collision with a Bf 109 flown by *Leutnant* Hans Kolbow of III / JG 51, but both pilots managed to return to their respective bases. A second Spitfire, flown by Pilot Officer James O'Meara, returned to base with heavy damage caused by *Oberleutnant* Arnold Lignitz of the 3rd *Staffel* / JG 51. *Unteroffizier* Walter Meisala was wounded in the encounter between the two sides, but managed to nurse his damaged aircraft back to make a force landing in France. A Hurricane from 32 Squadron was also shot down by *Unteroffizier* Maximilian Mayer from III / JG 51, crashing at Hougham. The pilot, Sergeant Guy Turner, was badly burned and admitted to Dover Hospital.

20th July 1940

The Dover Straits remained shrouded with cloud, but this cleared as the day passed, giving way to bright intervals. During the afternoon, a comparatively large convoy, CW7 (codename *Bosom*), comprising 29 merchant vessels and three escorts, began the transit from North Foreland towards Dover.

Air Vice-Marshall Keith Park, commander of 11 Group which covered the southeast of England, London and the Channel area, realised that the convoy must have presented a tempting target for the *Luftwaffe*. This had already been demonstrated by the efforts made the previous day to attack the convoy as it assembled in the Thames Estuary. Despite his often-voiced concern over sending his pilots on sorties over the waters of the Channel and Thames Estuary, he was under instructions to provide Channel convoys with sufficient cover to hinder damaging attacks. With this in mind, *Bosom* was patrolled by Hurricanes from 32 and 615 squadrons with two Spitfire Squadrons (65 and 610) in a high cover position.

As the convoy passed Deal, it came under attack from the 3rd *Staffel* of *Erprobungsgruppe 210* under *Oberleutnant* Otto Hintze. His unit, unlike the rest of this experimental group which was equipped with the Messerschmitt Bf 110, had been conducting operational trials on the use of the Bf 109 as a fighter-bomber.

The employment of the Bf 109 in this role proved confusing both for the British radar plotters and the Observer Corps. Despite the attack profile of the Bf 109 fighter bomber being significantly different from the steep attack dives used by the Ju 87s, they were frequently mistaken for the gull-winged Stukas, whose awe-inspiring reputation made such misidentifications partially understandable. Despite their approach across the Channel being made at much higher speeds than either Stukas or medium bomber formations, fighter-bomber raids were continually interpreted as fighters on offensive sweeps, seen as a limited threat to strategic targets such as shipping, radar or coastal facilities.

Leutnant Horst Marx poses in front of one of the Messerschmitt Bf 109 E-4 fighter-bombers that equipped the 3rd Staffel of Erprobungsgruppe 210. (Via Goss)

It's no surprise therefore that the attack by *Oberleutnant* Otto Hintze's 3rd *Staffel* was neither generally recorded, nor intercepted. On this occasion, the bombs that the Bf 109s dropped also appear to have caused no damage to the convoy's ships.

Bosom was attacked again in the late afternoon some 10 miles off Dover by Stukas from *Hauptmann* Anton Keil's II / StG 1, with a heavy escort of Bf 109s from JG 51. The German escorts had mixed success in diverting the RAF fighters away from the Stukas, four of which were damaged but all of which succeeded in limping back to France with only one NCO wounded.

The dive-bombers completed their attack on the convoy, sinking the British collier *Pulborough 1* (960 tons) and damaging the British vessel *Westown* (710 tons), which had to be towed into Dover. Two larger Norwegian freighters would also be damaged before the convoy finally reached the West Country.

The vulnerability of the Royal Navy escorts in waters so close to the German air bases in north France was also amply demonstrated during this engagement. Anton Keil's Ju 87s managed to damage the destroyer *HMS Beagle* with bomb splinters from near misses, but a second destroyer, *HMS Brazen,* was hit and damaged so badly that the vessel sank under tow the following day. At the Admiralty, this started a process of re-assessment of the strategic value of basing the 4th Destroyer Flotilla at Dover as an anti-invasion deterrent. This would eventually lead to the flotilla's withdrawal from Dover due to the losses incurred on the 20th of July and the days that followed.

JG 51 suffered two Bf 109 casualties in this engagement, with the loss of one pilot. One aircraft was abandoned before it crashed on the beach near Audinghem, but the pilot, *Oberfeldwebel* Oskar Sicking, was killed despite baling out. The second crashed into the sea off the French coast and the pilot was rescued by the *Seenotflugkommando*, this possibly being the aircraft shot down by Flight Lieutenant Pete Brothers, the flight commander of "B" Flight from Squadron Leader John "Baron" Worrall's 32 Squadron. This was the fourth kill claimed by Pete Brothers who finished the Battle of Britain with a total of 12 German aircraft falling under his guns over that period.

At the same time, 32 Squadron lost two Hurricanes with one pilot posted as missing. Squadron Leader Worrall was the pilot who survived and his combat report described the incident.

> *I was leading Green Section on a convoy patrol off Dover from 17.00 to 18.00 hours. At 1740, Sapper (Biggin Hill control) told me Blue Section was joining me, also enemy aircraft between 10,000 and 20,000 feet were approaching the convoy. Almost at once, I spotted them and ordering Green Section line astern attacked the first Ju 87 just as he was starting his dive. Despite the fact that I had throttled right back, I overtook him after a two second burst. I turned and took on another but had to break off as I was attacked by an Me 110. I then lost the 110 and saw the Ju 87s bombing a destroyer. They finished bombing and made for home. I attacked the nearest who started smoking. I had to break off again as I was attacked by a 109. I could not see or find the 109 so I attacked a third Ju 87 which started to smoke. I was just about to fire another burst when I saw tracer going over my port wing. I immediately broke away and felt bullets entering the aircraft from behind which were stopped by armour plating. Then two cannon shells hit, one in the engine and one in the gravity tank. I turned for home and the engine petered out just too far away from Hawkinge. I had to make a crash-landing in a small field half-mile to the east of the drome. Almost immediately she went up in a slow fire giving me about half a minute to get out.*

A third Hurricane was damaged, but the wounded pilot managed to return to base. These were all victims of the Bf 109s from JG 51, as was a Spitfire from 610 Squadron whose tail was shot away over Hawkinge, but the slightly wounded pilot managed to bale out, landing at Lydden.

21st – 23rd July 1940

Despite comparatively fair, hazy weather over the south of England and the Channel area, there was a lull in daylight air operations over Kent and the southeast between the 21st and the 23rd of July.

German reconnaissance sorties continued throughout Britain and the convoy traffic in the Channel and the Dover Straits came in for its share of attention. There were no recorded casualties related to operations over Kent but there was more persistent activity in the southwest.

24th July 1940

While the weather in the Channel and the Dover Straits deteriorated the following day, the *Luftwaffe* continued its campaign against shipping in the Dover and Thames Estuary areas.

Early morning saw 54 Squadron scrambling from Hornchurch to intercept the first raids aimed at ships as they gathered off North Foreland and the Downs. Two sections of "B" Flight's Spitfires climbed to intercept a formation of Dornier Do 17 bombers from Johannes Fink's KG 2, shepherded by a heavy escort of Bf 109 fighters. The Spitfires made contact with the bomber formation which jettisoned its bomb load and returned to France without any casualties. Two Spitfires from 54 Squadron were damaged during this early encounter, but both managed to return to base for repair. A third Spitfire from 64 Squadron based at Kenley was also damaged as the bomber formation withdrew over the Goodwin Sands, but it also returned to base.

On its first operational sortie since moving to their new airfield, a cleared rye field in the Pas de Calais, III / JG 52 provided close escort for the Stukas from Bruno Lörzer's II *Fliegercorps* from the Pas de Calais as they crossed the Channel to attack shipping and other targets around Dover shortly before midday. The fighters and dive-bombers rendezvoused over Boulogne and headed north towards England through the murky clouds. Among the pilots of the 8th *Staffel* / JG 52 was 22 year-old *Leutnant* Günther Rall, somewhat uncomfortable in his struggle to match the slow speed of the Stukas.

As the *Luftwaffe* formation reached Dover and the Stukas began their attack, Spitfires from 54 and 610 Squadrons appeared without warning from the clouds and the Bf 109s from JG 52 became embroiled in a fierce dogfight. Despite combat experience in the Battle for France before the Dunkirk evacuation, none of the German fighter pilots could understand how their positions were compromised in such poor visibility. The effectiveness of Dowding's radar and sector control system in locating threats approaching over the Channel was an unsettling revelation that gradually dawned on the *Luftwaffe* as the Battle of Britain intensified.

Any semblance of cohesion within the German fighter formation was lost as each pilot struggled individually to evade or attack the British fighters. There were no recorded British casualties, although two of the German pilots claimed to have shot down a Spitfire.

However, between 1130 and 1230 hours, JG 52 lost four aircraft in the sea off Margate, all four pilots being killed, including *Hauptmann* Wolf-Dietrich von Houwald, the *Gruppenkommandeur, Oberleutnant* Herbert Fermer, the *Staffelkapitän* of the 7th *Staffel* and *Oberleutnant* Lothar Ehrlich, the *Staffelkapitän* of the 8th *Staffel*. The loss of such senior officers in the *Jagdwaffe* during one sortie was an early sign of problems that would continue to plague the German fighter units operating over Britain and the English Channel throughout the conflict.

Flight Lieutenant John Ellis had been leading the formation of Spitfires from 610 Squadron and his combat report is believed to describe the fate of a 7th *Staffel* Bf 109 flown by *Gefreiter* Erich Frank which crashed in the sea off Margate at 1215 hours.

> *I was leading three sections of 610 Squadron on a patrol at 12,000' off Dover on 24/7/40. We took off at about 1115. At 1130 I sighted three Me 109's three thousand feet above us and flying west in the opposite direction to us. As I had to use full throttle to catch the e/a the remaining two sections got left behind. The formation of 109's broke up on being attacked and I singled out one of them. I opened fire at 200 yds. on the first burst and he immediately rolled on to his back and dived vertically, he then pulled out and proceeded to climb practically vertically. He carried out this manoeuvre four times and each time I got in a good burst while he was climbing. Throughout these evolutions bluish smoke was coming from a point about a foot from each wing tip. On his final climb I got in a good burst of roughly 5 seconds from dead astern, the Me 109 suddenly belched forth clouds of black smoke and white smoke, turned on its back and spiralled down in a vertical dive. It looked to be completely out of control. I followed the burning aircraft down until it entered a cloud at 3000' still going down almost vertically. F/O Wilson & Sgt Arnfield saw this e/a go down.*

When JG 52 returned to France and realised that three of their senior officers had not returned, it was an understandably serious blow to morale. *Leutnant* Günther Rall was appointed *Staffelkapitän* of the 8th *Staffel* the next day, but during the Battle of Britain he was not to achieve the high level of successes he managed in other theatres later in the war. This was perhaps partly because III /JG 52 spent only ten days on the Channel Front before being withdrawn back to Germany due to their high casualty rates. The unit was transferred in October 1940 to Roumania to protect the Ploesti oil fields. Günther Rall died in 2009, having survived the end of the war to become one of Germany's highest scoring fighter aces with 275 kills, mostly on the Eastern Front and in defence of Germany. Even to this day, this made him the third highest scoring fighter pilot ever behind two other *Jagdwaffe* fighter pilots that had amassed higher scores, both mainly in the Russian theatre.

Shortly after midday, the Spitfires from 54 Squadron were called again to intercept another group of 18 Do 17 bombers which were focusing their attention on the ships that had been gathering in the Thames Estuary.

On this occasion, the bombers were under the protection of JG 26 (*Schlageter*), which had recently completed its transfer into the Pas de Calais area to strengthen the single engine fighter force already operating from bases in the area. The *Geschwader Stab* and I *Gruppe* had moved to Audembert on the 15th of July, with II *Gruppe* and III *Gruppe* joining them on the 21st of July at Marquise and Caffiers respectively. Both these last two locations had ironically been used as British air bases during the First World War.

Hauptmann Erich Noack, the *Gruppenkommandeur* of II / JG 26 led an offensive sweep ahead of the bombers, while Adolf Galland's III *Gruppe* was looking after the bombers' escort needs. Noack's unit had not yet reached full operational status after the recent move and was seriously under strength, with only ten machines able to take part in this sortie, less than one-third of its established strength. As they approached the British coast at Dover, he spotted what he thought was a large force of Spitfires above their position and decided to abort the sweep and return to Marquise. As it was, Spitfires were indeed overhead, 610 Squadron operating nine aircraft over Dover at this time. As he returned to land back at Marquise, Noack made an approach that was too high and, as he pulled up to go round for a second attempt, he stalled, crashed and was killed instantly. The following day, he was succeeded by *Oberleutnant* Karl Ebbighausen, who led II / JG 26 until his own death off Dover on the 16th of August 1940.

The bombers and their fighter escort continued towards the Thames Estuary where they ran into the whole of 54 Squadron, which was soon joined by the Spitfires from 65 Squadron operating from Manston. While the Spitfires prevented the bombers from damaging the ships in the Thames Estuary below, the bombers returned to France without loss. The Spitfires from the two British squadrons were blocked by the 40 Bf 109s from the remainder of JG 26, and a frantic dogfight took place over the Dover Straits with losses on both sides.

Five days after his promotion to *Major*, Adolf Galland was credited with shooting down a Spitfire from 54 Squadron, his 15th victim, during this engagement. It was piloted by Pilot Officer John Allen, himself credited with eight victories. Allen's engine had been damaged off Margate, but as he attempted to reach Manston at 1245 hours, his aircraft stalled and crashed in flames close to the Old Charles Inn at Cliftonville, near Margate. Two other 54 Squadron Spitfires were damaged, with one of the pilots slightly wounded.

JG 26 didn't have it all their own way. At 1300 hours, 38-year old *Oberleutnant* Werner Bartels, the Technical Officer of III / JG 26, was shot down and seriously wounded in an attack by one of the Spitfires, causing him to force land close to the Broadstairs/Margate railway line in a wheat field at Northdown, Kent.

It's believed he was shot down by Squadron Leader Henry Sawyer, the commander of 65 Squadron, then based at Hornchurch. Like many downed German aircraft that were not completely destroyed as they came down, his Bf 109 E-1 was later put on exhibition in Croydon, as well as other parts of the country, to encourage the public to contribute funds for the war effort. Bartels, a former test pilot and engineer, was a popular pilot in JG 26. In a curiously ironic move, he was repatriated to Germany due to the severity of his injuries in 1943, later becoming involved in the Messerschmitt Me 262 jet development programme.

Oberleutnant Werner Bartels' Messerschmitt Bf 109 E-1 under examination by RAF Intelligence after the force landing close to the Broadstairs-Margate railway line, just visible in the background.

Shortly after this incident, *Leutnant* Josef Schauff of the 8th *Staffel* was also shot down over Margate. He baled out of his doomed Bf 109 E-4, but his parachute failed and he fell to his death as his aircraft crashed in Margate's Byron Avenue. Such parachute failures became a tragic but regular feature of the aerial combat over the coming weeks, affecting both sides of the conflict.

As the day ended, it was a chastened Johannes Fink who absorbed the news of the loss of so many important *Jagdwaffe* leaders including two *Gruppenkommandeurs*, two *Staffelkapitäns* and one popular Headquarters' Flight Technical Officer. The Channel battles were already demonstrating that promotion comes quickly when heavy losses are incurred among the higher-ranking pilots.

25th July 1940

It was a fine Thursday in the Dover Straits with light north north-westerly winds and some haze. Convoy CW8 *(Bacon)* steamed on its westerly course and suffered heavy attacks off Deal. With all shipping movements in the Dover straits clear to German observers through the mobile *Freya* radar unit at Cap Blanc Nez, Johannes Fink decided it was time to send a strong signal to the British Admiralty that it was unsafe to continue to send convoy traffic through the Channel in daylight. *Luftwaffe* reconnaissance flights had identified *Bacon's* 21 coasters and armed trawler escorts as a tempting target in support of German efforts to prevent British convoys passing along the Channel.

Having watched the convoy slowly appearing from North Foreland in the early afternoon, Fink sent 57 Ju 87s to attack the convoy in three waves accompanied by a heavy escort of Bf 109s. Some of the fighter escorts approached the convoy at sea level rather than from their preferred high altitude, strafing the convoy's ships and diverting the ships' gunners' attention away from the Stukas as they peeled off to begin their diving attacks.

In order to maximise the accuracy of dive-bombing attacks on mobile targets such as ships that were taking evasive manoeuvres, the *Stukas* would use their dive brakes to follow a steeper attack profile than was possible without the dive brakes. The negative side of using the speed brakes was that the pull-out radius was tighter and the Stukas had to strain to pick up speed to climb away, a position which made them vulnerable targets. German fighters found it difficult enough to match the level cruising speed of the Ju 87 without stalling, let alone following the slower dive-bombers during their diving attack. Arguably, with some German fighters already operating near sea level, there was some hope that these would also be able to offer protection to the Stukas as they slowly regained height and the mutual protection afforded by their *Ketten's* defensive armament. This was entirely at odds with virtually all fighter pilots' tactics where height advantage offered both an overall view of the tactical situation and the opportunity to dive, make a quick attack and zoom back to altitude.

It appears to have been *Hauptmann* Anton Keil's II / StG 1 (until earlier in July III / StG 51) and *Hauptmann* Bernd von Brauchitsh's IV / LG 1 that were responsible for the attacks on the convoy. These resulted in damage to the British flag cement carrier *Summity* (554 tons) which was beached near Dover. The Danish flag *Gronland* (1,264 tons) was also damaged and later sank in Dover harbour, while two other British flag ships, the *Newminster* (967 tons) and the *Tamworth* (1,332 tons), were both towed into Dover harbour after being hit by the Stukas.

The raid was intercepted by Hurricanes from 32 and 615 Squadrons, reinforced by Spitfires from 54 Squadron, but the German escorts managed to keep the RAF pilots from wreaking the damage they had hoped for on the dive-bombers.

Nearer 1430 hours, 40 Ju 88s, escorted by 50 Bf 109s approached the convoy but were intercepted by Hurricanes from 111 Squadron and Spitfires from 54 and 64 squadrons. As 54 Squadron climbed to engage the German formation, Pilot Officer Douglas Turkey-George described their encounter which resulted in the loss of one of his colleagues, Flight Lieutenant Basil "Wonky" Way.

> *The 109s coming at us from above as we still struggled for height – Way*
> *being hit and falling away out of sight. I remember the 109 attacking me*
> *from the port side, my trying to turn in towards him, the loud bangs of*

his cannon shells striking my Spitfire as he hit me from an almost full deflection angle; and even through the pounding fear that I felt, admiring his marksmanship. A few seconds later, with my aeroplane miraculously still answering apparently normally to the controls, finding myself behind two Me 109s, aligning my sight on one, pressing the gun button – and the guns failing to fire; then diving out of the fight to return to base.

A Junkers Ju 87 B from the 6th Staffel of Anton Keil's II / StG 1 in north France with a full load of bombs waiting for the next sortie against Channel shipping.

Turkey-George's faith in the dependability of his damaged Spitfire was misplaced and he was forced to make a crash-landing near Dover at 1500 hours, walking away relieved and unhurt.

The convoy plodded westwards, the sky above witnessing a confused dogfight as different groups of fighters met, with the British pilots trying vainly to get through to the bombers attacking the ships below. With less worries about the fuel limitations than would later become a problem for the Bf 109 pilots as the conflict moved to the outer reaches of their fuel range, the *Jagdwaffe* pilots were able to protect the bulk of the bomber force, as well as inflicting painful casualties among the RAF squadrons they were facing.

This was not without some sacrifice. By the end of the day, four Bf 109s had been lost in the waters of the Channel with their pilots killed or missing. It was another bad day for Günther Rall's III / JG 52, since three of the pilots lost were from this unit. Yet again it was the senior pilots that suffered, with one *Staffelkapitän* killed and a *Staffelführer* missing. A fifth aircraft from the 8th *Staffel* was shot down by Spitfires from 610 Squadron and crash-landed near Deal where the pilot, *Unteroffizier* Max Reiss, was taken prisoner. Despite claims from the convoy's escorts of several dive-bombers shot down, only two Stukas from II / StG 1 failed to return to France, and what evidence remains suggests these had also been victims of the British fighters that were trying to shield the convoy.

For 11 Group, however, the day finished on a sad note, highlighting the overwhelming numerical superiority that the *Jagdwaffe* regularly had in its favour over the Channel convoys. Earlier in the day, a Hurricane from 32 Squadron had been damaged by German fighters over Dover, but the pilot was able to force land the aircraft close by at 1250 hours. As the afternoon's sorties progressed, six Spitfires were shot down and four more damaged, with four pilots killed and one wounded. A fifth pilot also died later as a result of the day's engagement. This was Sub-Lieutenant Francis Dawson- Paul of 64 Squadron based at Kenley, who was severely wounded and crashed into the sea. He was picked up by a German *Schnellboot* but his wounds were so serious that he died five days later.

The attacks on the convoy from the air were supplemented by artillery fire from the heavy guns on the French coast, as well as attacks from *Kriegsmarine* E-boats (*Schnellbooten – S-Boot*). In order to provide convoy CW8 with escorts, the Royal Navy sent out two destroyers from Dover's 4th Destroyer Flotilla to chase the German boats back to France. While they were successful in this, they were arguably over-zealous in approaching Calais too closely. Johannes Fink promptly dispatched the Bf 110s from *Erprobungsgruppe 210*, as well as some Ju 87s and to attack the British destroyers.

Both were seriously damaged, with *HMS Boreas* hit twice on the bridge and suffering 50 casualties killed or wounded. The other destroyer, *HMS Brilliant*, was also hit twice, but it was their lucky day since the bombs that hit them failed to explode and both ships retreated to the relative safety of Dover harbour. Following this action and the loss of the destroyer *HMS Codrington* in Dover harbour on the 27th of July, the Admiralty concluded that the port had finally become too dangerous to use as a base for an anti-invasion destroyer flotilla, and the remainder of the 4th Destroyer Flotilla were withdrawn northwards.

This was not the only redeployment of forces that stemmed from the German actions on the 25th of July. Hornchurch's 54 Squadron, which had by then been involved in continuous sorties for the previous three weeks, were sent for a rest to Catterick in the North. Over the 24th and 25th of July, the squadron had lost four pilots killed or wounded, with five Spitfires lost and four more damaged. Protecting the convoys along Britain's south coast, in particular through the vulnerable Dover Straits, had become a costly business for 11 Group which bore the brunt of this, exposing both pilots and machines to the dangers of operations over the inhospitable Channel.

The transfer of tired or depleted squadrons from 11 Group to quieter sectors of Fighter Command was a process that Keith Park, Air Officer Commanding 11 Group, would continue to use throughout the Battle of Britain with the support of Fighter Command's Commander-in-Chief, Air Chief Marshall Hugh Dowding. It allowed exhausted pilots that had been in action over the southeast time to rest and recuperate, as well as bringing untried or rested squadrons from the north or west to add their weight to what was becoming a daily struggle over the Channel and southeast England. As events later in the summer demonstrated, it was a double-edged sword since it exposed inexperienced squadrons to the hectic combat conditions that progressively worsened over the Home Counties.

By the time convoy *Bacon* reached Falmouth on the 29th of July, many of its vessels had been sunk and damaged. There is some question as to the actual numbers, but up to ten vessels were probably lost, with at least five more damaged by the attacks of the combined German forces that had been sent against it. The Germans had readily demonstrated that sending daylight convoy traffic through the Channel was a dangerous gambit with the *Luftwaffe* beginning to prove its domination in the skies over the Dover Straits.

26th – 27th July 1940

Poor visibility with heavy cloud and rain covered the Dover Straits on the 26th of July. German attention was focussed in the western Channel as convoy CW8 (*Bacon*) moved past the Isle of Wight and Portland. Friday the 27th of July was fair with more cloud further west in the Channel and some rain over the Midlands and the North Sea.

In the Channel area, there were two attacks on Dover harbour. In the west, Stukas continued their assault against the convoy *Bacon*, and the Bf 110s of *Erprobungsgruppe 210* attacked a convoy off the east coast, near Harwich.

With reduced convoy traffic passing through the Dover Straits, Johannes Fink turned his attention to the Royal Navy's presence in the area. Dover became the focus of more bombing attacks during the day, one of these hitting the harbour as well as Dover Barracks.

With the Bf 110s from the 1st and 2nd *Staffeln* of *Erprobungsgruppe 210* dispatched against the east coast convoys, it was the Bf 109 *Jabos* of the 3rd *Staffel* that were involved in the bombings around Dover. At 1430 hours, *Leutnant* Otto Hintze led 10 of his fighter-bombers in an attack that added more damage to the dock facilities and the surrounding area, one of their victims being a steamer off the coast near Sandgate. It was a busy afternoon for his *Staffel* since they were back shortly around 1800 hours when they made landfall at Dungeness and caused more damage with their 250 kg bombs,

The major casualty of this raid was the destroyer *HMS Codrington* and the depot ship *HMS Sandhurst*. The *Codrington* had been undergoing a long-overdue boiler clean moored alongside the *Sandhurst* in the submarine basin. The destroyer received a near-miss that was sufficient to break her back. Her stern half was later beached on the seafront by the White Cliff Hotel and remained there until 1947 when it was towed to Chatham. This was the final signal for the Admiralty to withdraw the flotilla northwards, away from the immediate danger of attack from units based in North France.

The *Sandhurst,* loaded with torpedoes, ammunition and fuel, was heavily damaged and caught fire, threatening an explosion that would have caused terrible damage and casualties over a wide area of the harbour and the surrounding town. Four fire pumps from the local Fire Brigade, assisted by hoses from a nearby tugboat, fought to stop the fire spreading and to contain the potential disaster that threatened. Frank

Illingworth, a member of the Auxiliary Fire Service, had ridden his bike to the fire station when it became clear an attack was in progress, later recalled:

A pall of smoke rises from HMS Sandhurst with the crippled destroyer HMS Codrington moored alongside in Dover Harbour's submarine basin on the 29th of July 1940.

> *The decks were steaming, the side plates sizzling, but eventually the fire was brought under control. Tired, hungry, blackened and scorched, we returned to the station.*

As a prelude to the progressive movement of increasing numbers of Bf 109s to the Pas de Calais area demanded by the impending start of the next stage of Göring's aerial assault on Britain, the command structure of the forces arrayed in North France underwent some changes. *Onkel* Theo Oesterkamp, until then the *Kommodore* of JG 51, which had been the foundation for the fighter strength located around Calais, was assigned the title of *Jagdfliegerführer 2* (*Jafu 2*), assuming a role that was to control the tactical disposition of the fighter units under *Luftflotte* 2. It was an essential, if sometimes confusing, responsibility.

His place as *Kommodore* of JG 51 was taken by *Major* Werner Mölders, an inspirational leader and aerial tactician, the first of the younger group of experienced fighter pilots who would replace older unit commanders in the days and weeks that followed. *"Vati"* (Daddy) Mölders had made his reputation earlier, emerging from the Spanish Civil War as the *Luftwaffe's* highest scoring fighter pilot. During the invasion of France and the Low Countries, he had been *Staffelkapitän*, then *Gruppenkommandeur*, in JG 53 (*Pik As* – Ace of Spades), towards the end of which operation he was shot down by French aircraft and taken prisoner. After the armistice between Germany and France towards the end of June, he had been repatriated and promoted from *Hauptmann* to the rank of *Major* when he took over JG 51, already with a tally of 39 victories.

28th July 1940

The weather was fine during the early part of the day before clouding over later. *Luftwaffe* activity was concentrated on the Channel around Dover, as well as the on the east coast of Britain.

A large raid developed at 1200 hours but this was turned back halfway across the Dover Straits. A second attack was launched two hours later with 50 fighters protecting 50 bombers, but there was no record of any bombs being dropped.

In the ensuing clash, the Bf 109s of JG 51 and JG 26 were intercepted by Hurricanes from 111 and 257 squadrons together with Spitfires from 41 and 74 squadrons and both sides suffered casualties. Two Spitfires and one Hurricane were destroyed, with three further Spitfires damaged, one pilot killed and three wounded. For the *Luftwaffe*, the situation could have been much more disastrous. As the Spitfires of 41 and 74 squadrons engaged Mölders' Bf 109s, three of JG 51's aircraft were hit, one crashing into the sea, brought down by Pilot Officer George "Ben" Bennions of 41 Squadron. The other two Bf 109s were only damaged, although one was written off when it force landed on the French coast with its pilot wounded.

Werner Mölders was flying his first mission as JG 51's *Kommodore*, with elements of I and II / JG 51 escorting the bombers attacking Dover. High above the bombers and their close escort, Adolf Galland was operating as top cover with III / JG 26. With the escort mission over, Mölders instructed his unit to return to base but continued over the area of operations, alone apart from his wingman, *Oberleutnant* Erich Kircheis. In doing this, he was ignoring Herman Göring's instructions that no pilots of the *Kommodore* rank should operate over England, having already lost too many of his experienced high-ranking pilots in the preceding weeks of action over the Channel.

With his hunter's instincts and excellent eyesight, Mölders caught sight of a section of three Spitfires flying some 3,000 – 6,000 feet below, apparently unaware of the potential threat above. As his *Kommodore* manoeuvred above the British pilots to get into their blind spot in the sun, Kircheis was keeping an eye on any other aircraft above and behind, as the wingman was expected to do. He spotted two groups approaching them from above and behind but, on warning Mölders of their position, was told by his leader that they were German aircraft. As they came closer, it became obvious they were not. They were British reinforcements, intent on helping the Spitfires that Mölders was stalking. JG 51's *Kommodore* nevertheless pressed home his attack and shot one down, probably Flying Officer Tony Lovell of 41 Squadron, who was wounded in the thigh and crashed his damaged Spitfire at Manston at 1435 hours.

Ground crew ensure Werner Mölders' seat straps are tight as he prepares to take off for a sortie during the summer of 1940 when he was Gruppen Kommandeur of JG 51. (Via Goss)

Mölders and Kircheis were forced to make wild evasive manoeuvres to avoid the attentions of the other Spitfires that were all over them, and the pair lost contact with each other in the process. Kircheis recalled diving away quickly and losing 12,000 feet in the classic Bf 109 diving escape, returning to base near Calais with a couple of hits in the engine. Mölders was less fortunate, his aircraft taking numerous hits, including some in the cockpit area, which wounded him in the left knee. He had probably been attacked by another of 41 Squadron's pilots, Flight Lieutenant John Webster, but managed to nurse his damaged aircraft back to the French coast where he made a force landing. He later described the incident.

> *Suddenly I see three English fighter planes, and behind them a swarm of Spitfires in the smoke. These Spitfires fly a bit lower. I take on the Kette. As I near, both outermost Spitfires turn, the middle one flies on. I set myself behind him and shoot from a distance of 60 m. The right side catches fire immediately, thick smoke and flames come from the plane that disappears below. I pull up and see a swarm of Spitfires, 8 – 10,*

behind me. I am in great shock. Only one thing can help me here: push through the middle of the swarm! I sweep through, the front planes cannot reach me any longer, but one behind me is watching very carefully.

He shoots and hits. It is rattling inside my plane. Shots in the cooling system, sides and gas tank. I retreat while the sides are turning and continue at 700 kph towards the Channel. The Spitfires are after me and my trail of smoke. Thank God the motor holds out. Then Oberleutnant Leppla comes to help. He observed the fuss. He attacked the Spitfire that was ready to attack. After a few seconds he crashed below covered in smoke. When I reached the coast the engine began to grumble. During landing, the landing gear did not come out. I made a smooth belly landing. When I wanted to climb out of the plane, my legs were unusually weak. I saw traces of blood. The results of the examination in the Military Hospital: three fractures in the thigh, one in the knee joint and one in the left foot. In the heat of combat, I didn't notice a thing.

Unaware that he had been injured until he emerged from his damaged Bf 109, Mölders noticed his blood-soaked trousers and he was rushed to hospital. He was taken off flying duties for some length of time. It was a lucky escape for one of the *Jagdwaffe*'s top scorers and rising stars and, while he was hospitalised, the unfortunate Erich Kircheis doubtless had to withstand Göring's wrath for failing to protect one of the *Luftwaffe*'s more valuable assets. Mölders finally rejoined JG 51 on the 7th of August.

29th July 1940

The Air Ministry issued its communiqué clarifying their position on the *Seenotflugkommando* floatplanes that bore civil markings and the Red Cross, confirming they would be treated as hostile if they ventured into operational areas around Britain. The view was that these aircraft, in addition to their humanitarian use rescuing downed aircrew from the sea, were being used for reconnaissance and other duties that assisted German war aims.

Enemy aircraft bearing civilian markings and marked with the Red Cross have recently flown over British ships at sea and in the vicinity of the British coast, and they are being employed for purposes which His Majesty's Government cannot regard as being consistent with the privileges generally accorded to the Red Cross.

His Majesty's Government desire to accord to ambulance aircraft reasonable facilities for the transportation of sick and wounded, in accordance with the Red Cross Convention, and aircraft engaged in the direct evacuation of the sick and wounded will be respected, provided they comply with the relevant provisions of the Convention.

His Majesty's Government are unable, however, to grant immunity to such aircraft flying over areas in which operations are in progress on land or at sea, or approaching British or Allied territory, or territory in British occupation, or British or Allied ships.

Ambulance aircraft which do not comply with the above requirements will do so at their own risk and peril.

It was a decision that created huge controversy among the *Luftwaffe* crews who viewed it as a barbaric decision, having an impact on both sides since these aircraft picked up downed airmen irrespective of the flag under which they flew.

With fair weather throughout Britain and hazy visibility around Dover and the Channel, the British RDF system detected a raid building up over North France in the early morning, which turned out to be almost 50 Stukas from II / StG 1and IV / LG1 with an escort of some 50 Bf 109s from JG 51. The incoming raiders were intercepted at altitudes of between 5,000 and 15,000 ft before they could begin their bombing runs. The Dover AA gunners kept up a heavy rate of fire even when the British aircraft were engaging.

The first was shortly after 0700 hours when *HMS Gulzar*, a motorised yacht fitted for minesweeping duty, was sunk in the harbour and on fire. The burning fuel on the harbour surface affected the already-damaged *HMS Sandhurst*. For their bravery and efforts during the fire on *HMS Sandhurst* on the 29th of July, three George Medals were awarded to senior members of the Dover Fire Brigade and the Auxiliary Fire Service and commendations were awarded for bravery to six other firemen from the two services.

Overhead, there were heavy casualties on both sides, with the AA gunners being credited with bringing down two Stukas, probably the two from the 11th *Staffel* / LG 1 that were shot down with all four crew members listed as killed or missing. Two further Stukas from II / StG 1 were written off as a result of this engagement, one lost in the Channel with its two crew members rescued, the other crash-landing at St Inglevert in France with one NCO wounded. A third Ju 87 from the unit returned to base in France, again with one of the crew wounded. The fighters of JG 51 didn't escape this action unscathed, two Bf 109s limping back to crash on the French coast, killing both pilots.

On the British side, two pilots were killed, one from 56 Squadron whose Hurricane crashed and exploded in the sea off Dover after being shot down by one of JG 51's Bf 109s. Also lost during this action was a pilot from 41 Squadron whose Spitfire had been hit by return fire from the Stukas and crashed in the Channel. The pilot was recorded as missing.

Manston's 41 Squadron had four other Spitfires damaged during this engagement, two being written off when they landed and the other two capable of being

The following day brought fair weather with slightly above-average temperatures throughout the country, although there was some haze in the Channel and the Dover Straits. The *Luftwaffe* sent a variety of reconnaissance aircraft across the Channel, some of which were directed into the North Sea where some isolated raids followed. In the late afternoon, around 15 Bf 109s from II / JG 51 headed for Dover and 11 Group controllers scrambled five squadrons to intercept them. In the event, only 74 Squadron from Hornchurch found the German formation, suffering from the ensuing battle when two Spitfires were lost with their pilots killed and a third machine was damaged. There were no recorded casualties from JG 51.

Following the withdrawal of the 4th Destroyer Flotilla from Dover and the decimation of the westbound convoy on the 25th of July, the German aim of stopping convoy traffic in the Channel had effectively been achieved. At the same time, it was evident to *Luftwaffe* High Command that damaging RAF Fighter Command sufficiently to guarantee air superiority over the Channel and southern England was more difficult than earlier expectations had suggested. It would demand much greater fighter strength than had been possible with the units so far based around Calais.

As the groundwork was being laid to extend the Luftwaffe's attacks further inland against RAF airfields and aircraft factories, no fewer than eight additional *Gruppen* were to join JG 51, JG 26, JG 52 and JG 3 at bases around Calais and Boulogne between the end of July and the 8th of August 1940. *Adlertag* (Eagle Day), the opening of the new stage of the assault against Britain, was not far off, waiting for the next window of continuous fair weather before it could be implemented.

1st – 10th August 1940

In the Dover Straits and the Channel the weather became warmer but the skies were overcast, with low cloud dispersing as the first day of August passed. This reduced aerial activity, with little of significance occurring in the area apart from some night-time mine-laying by the *Luftwaffe* in the Thames Estuary.

Hitler issued Directive No. 17, the broad outline for the continued conduct of the war against Britain across the Channel.

In order to establish the necessary conditions for the final conquest of England I intend to intensify air and sea warfare against the English homeland. I therefore order as follows:
1. The German Air Force is to overpower the English Air Force with all the forces at its command, in the shortest possible time. The attacks are to be directed primarily against flying units, their ground installations, and their supply organisations, but also against the aircraft industry, including that manufacturing anti-aircraft equipment.
2. After achieving temporary or local air superiority the air war is to be continued against ports, in particular against stores of food, and also against stores of provisions in the interior of the country.

Attacks on south coast ports will be made on the smallest possible scale, in view of our own forthcoming operations.

3. On the other hand, air attacks on enemy warships and merchant ships may be reduced except where some particularly favourable target happens to present itself, where such attacks would lend additional effectiveness to those mentioned in paragraph 2, or where such attacks are necessary for the training of air crews for further operations.

4. The intensified air warfare will be carried out in such a way that the Air Force can at any time be called upon to give adequate support to naval operations against suitable targets. It must also be ready to take part in full force in 'OperationSea Lion'.

5. I reserve to myself the right to decide on terror attacks as measures of reprisal.

6. The intensification of the air war may begin on or after 5th August. The exact time is to be decided by the Air Force after the completion of preparations and in the light of the weather.

The Navy is authorised to begin the proposed intensified naval war at the same time.

With this, Hitler delegated the decision on the timing for the next phase of the softening-up process to Göring and his colleagues, always subject to the vagaries of the weather. It signalled the end of the Channel battles, since it was clear by then that the *Luftwaffe* had indeed established a virtual no-go zone for convoy and related naval traffic in the Channel during daylight hours.

The decision by 11 Group's AOC, Keith Park, to limit the exposure of his pilots to the risk of loss over the dangerous waters of the Channel, also lent support to the *Luftwaffe's* conviction of control. Without the need to protect Channel convoy traffic, Park was content to allow German fighters to patrol the south coast without much interference, reacting more aggressively when the fighters were escorting bombers heading for potentially vulnerable targets on the coast itself and further inland.

So the first four days of the month saw comparatively little activity. In part, this was due to the weather which showed the contrary nature so typical of the summer over the Channel area. Cloud and drizzle created less than perfect conditions for mass raids, but the *Luftwaffe* maintained the established level of reconnaissance and night-time mine-laying sorties. In northern France and the Low Countries, the focus was on preparations for the start of the next stage of the air assault on Britain, *Adlertag* (Eagle Day), which would be aimed at achieving air superiority over southern England in preparation for the invasion.

With Hitler's Directive No. 17 giving Göring a free hand to spread the conflict inland from the Channel and release his *Luftwaffe* to inflict the same wholesale destruction that had been so successfully accomplished in Poland and the Low Countries, the uncooperative weather produced frustrating delays. While bad weather didn't hinder small raids of single bombers using the cloud and mist to evade interception, the mass raids that *Der Dicke* and his commanders were planning needed fair weather to ensure that large bomber formations could be employed with adequate fighter protection. Throughout the first ten days of August, it was as if the weather itself was conspiring to help Britain prepare for the onslaught that it knew was coming sooner or later.

Around Tonbridge, one raider dropped a large bundle of propaganda leaflets to which an explosive charge had been attached, fortunately finding one of the county's more strategic targets – a sewage farm. During another raid, an Observer Corps. post near Gravesend was put out of action by a bomb.

A flight of Hurricanes from 151 Squadron over southern Britain.

On the 5th of August there was some improvement in the weather although there was haze over the Channel. Despite the anxiety that it caused to both Dowding and Park, early morning saw Spitfires from Hornchurch's 65 Squadron patrolling four miles off the French coast near Calais, where they were attacked a group of Bf 109s from JG 51. The British aircraft succeeded in sending one of the Bf 109s into the sea, with a second limping back to France. More aircraft from both sides got involved, with Kenley's 64 Squadron losing a Spitfire together with its pilot, and a second being damaged, force landing at Hawkinge at 0900 hours. 65 Squadron also had one of its aircraft damaged by a Bf 109 from JG 54. The damaged Spitfire flown by Sergeant Walker made a force landing at Manston, having been set on fire with the pilot slightly wounded. Records suggest he had been the victim of *Oberleutnant* Reinhard Seiler of JG 54's 1st *Staffel*, which was in the process of moving into bases around Guines, south of Calais, to help strengthen the fighter force that would be needed to escort the mass bomber raids waiting for better weather.

During the early afternoon, a force of 30 - 40 German aircraft was detected hunting for shipping in the Channel and Spitfires from 41 Squadron at Hornchurch, together with Hurricanes from 151 Squadron based at North Weald, were sent to intercept them. They had limited success in this due to the hazy conditions. It turned out to be a short spell of reasonable weather with the adverse conditions returning, with low cloud and strong winds dominating the weather picture.

On the 7th of August, Convoy CW9, code named *Peewit*, made up of 25 merchant vessels and nine escorts, had formed up in the Thames Estuary and began its westbound passage to Falmouth. The hope was that it would pass through the vulnerable Dover Straits during night-time and this would prevent the losses caused by *Luftwaffe* daytime attacks. Convoy CW8, code named *Bacon*, which had left Southend on the 25th of July, had been the last convoy to transit the Straits in daylight and it had suffered heavy damage as it moved towards Falmouth.

However, German observers at Cap Blanc Nez had been tracking *Peewit*, not least by the inclusion in the convoy of six vessels towing kite balloons that were hoped to give some protection against aerial attack by dive-bombers. Armed with the information this provided, the decision was made to demonstrate finally to the British that the Channel was firmly under German control by obliterating the convoy by means of a combined naval, aerial and artillery assault as it made its journey through the Channel.

By the 8th of August, the Channel remained cloudy with showers and bright intervals. Convoy *Peewit* had left Southend the previous night and, as the new day dawned, it approached Beachy Head. A German E boat flotilla had been sent to wait for the convoy to pass Beachy Head and approach Newhaven. Early in the morning before sunrise, the E boats attacked off the Sussex port and the convoy was broken up, with three ships sunk and others damaged. Throughout the following days, a succession of heavy air attacks was made by Ju 87s with fighter escorts as the convoy pushed westwards. Four more merchantmen were sunk, six badly damaged, as were six armed escort vessels. The *Luftwaffe* had been instructed to exert maximum effort to ensure this convoy was destroyed, and *Peewit* ranks as the most heavily-attacked Channel convoy of the period. Out of the 23 vessels that originally gathered off Southend, only four merchant vessels managed to reach Falmouth. It was a demonstration that finally convinced the Admiralty that the whole of the Channel was unsafe for daylight convoy traffic.

While most of the air attacks occurred as the convoy plodded westwards along the Sussex and Hampshire coasts, there were continued incursions over the Dover Straits, particularly close to midday when Spitfires from 64, 65 and 610 Squadrons clashed with a collection of Bf 109s from both JG 51 and JG 26. At the end of the day, it was the RAF that had come off poorly, with four Spitfires destroyed and three pilots killed. The *Jagdwaffe* suffered only one fatality when one of its Bf 109s was shot down into the sea off Margate. *Oberleutnant* Willy Oehm from the 8th *Staffel* / JG 26 is believed to have been shot down by two pilots from 64 Squadron.

Shore defence personnel watch convoy traffic in the Channel under attack as the vessels pass through the Dover Straits.

Around the Isle of Wight, the groups of dive-bombers attacking the convoy, as well as their escorting single- and twin-engine fighters, suffered heavily at the hands of various fighter squadrons that 10 Group had scrambled to defend *Peewit*, assisted by some 11 Group squadrons. In all, the level of losses experienced by both sides ranked the 8th of August as the day of highest aerial losses since the fall of France, RAF losses amounting to 20 aircraft, with the *Luftwaffe* losing 30 in action over all of Britain.

On the 9th of August, the Channel was still covered with cloud and squally rain showers. After the previous day's hectic action around Convoy *Peewit* in the west, there was limited activity throughout the day. The *Luftwaffe* continued to send reconnaissance aircraft over many areas of the country in preparation for the major attacks that were to be launched when the weather conditions allowed.

All eyes in *Luftwaffe* High Command were on the Atlantic weather picture around the Azores which would indicate the future pattern over the all-important Channel area. Initial signs pointed to conditions that would allow the massive operations planned for *Adlertag* to be mounted on the 10th of August. As the day progressed however, the weather deteriorated again and the operations were delayed. The next weather window suggested the 13th of August as the best start date for these attacks.

The Dover balloon barrage was attacked during the day without success and three of 64 Squadron's Spitfires were damaged, requiring them to force land at Hawkinge.

True to the forecasts from the day before, the 10th of August saw cloudy conditions continuing over the Channel with further squally and thundery showers. There was little aerial activity apart from the continued reconnaissance missions mounted by various *Luftwaffe* aircraft types.

The airfield at West Malling was attacked by a lone Dornier Do 17 bomber around 0730 hours. This was the home of No. 26 (Army Co-operation) Squadron equipped with Westland Lysanders. The German aircraft had been tracked as it moved across from France, but the cloud obscured any visual contact until it dropped through the cloud base over the airfield, opened its bomb doors and made two passes, dropping a total of 14 bombs on and around the airfield. The airfield's facilities were in the process of being upgraded and the bombs that actually fell within the field's perimeter blew out the windows of some newly-constructed buildings and wounded building workers, one of whom died later from his injuries. Some of 26 Squadron's Lysanders were also damaged by machine gun fire from the Dornier which disappeared back into cloud before any of the airfield's defences could react.

11th August 1940

The day started with fair weather over the Channel and the Thames Estuary, but this deteriorated as the afternoon progressed.

With conditions initially looking good, the commanders of the two main German air groups facing the south of England decided to increase the pressure on RAF Fighter Command and Britain's naval installations. "Smiling Albert" Kesserling commanded *Luftflotte* 2 facing the Sussex, Kent and Essex coasts, while fearsome-looking Hugo Sperrle was in charge of *Luftflotte* 3 further west, which mounted operations mainly against southern and western Britain.

The heavier raids were to be made in the west, where a combined force of Heinkel He 111 and Junkers Ju 88 bombers was escorted by groups of Messerschmitt Bf 110 heavy fighters and their more agile Bf 109 relations. Their target was the naval base at Portland. Both 10 and 11 Group sent squadrons to intercept the raiders and after 1000 hours, a huge dogfight broke out with heavy losses on both sides.

During an early morning patrol over Dover, Pilot Officer Peter "Paddy" Stevenson of Hornchurch's 74 Squadron attacked a formation of Bf 109s on an offensive sweep at around 15,000 feet, shooting down one of the German fighters which crashed into the sea. After climbing to 23,000 feet, he dived to attack another enemy aircraft below him, but he was hit by cannon and machine gun fire from an unseen attacker. He managed to bale out of his doomed Spitfire but was blown out to sea. Even worse, his legs became entangled in the parachute shrouds and he was towed by the wind with his head underwater for what must have seemed several minutes before getting untangled. After a further hour in the water, he was finally picked up by a Motor Torpedo Boat, one of the few pilots fortunate enough to have been saved, doubly so since he was picked up by British forces rather than the roving German seaplanes and E-boats.

In an effort to draw Fighter Command's attention away from the heavier raid by Sperrle's force in the west, *Luftflotte 2* started the day by sending *Erprobungsgruppe 210* to attack Dover, where their twin-engine Bf 110 fighter-bombers scattered bombs over the town and docks. They were accompanied by the unit's 3rd *Staffel* with their single-engine Bf 109 fighters in fighter-bomber configuration, often confused with Ju 87 Stuka dive-bombers.

On this early morning sortie, they added to the confusion over the port by attacking the balloon barrage, managing to destroy three of these ungainly structures. This attack caught the population of the town by surprise since it was the first bombing raid on any scale that had hit the town itself, rather than the harbour. Since the radar plots showed the raid to be made up of high speed aircraft which were clearly fighters, rather than the slower and more worrying bombers, it was allowed to reach the English coast and return to France without interception. The speed of the raiders' approach to the target also gave British fighters little time to scramble from their forward bases and gain sufficient height to attack.

Groups of *Jagdwaffe* fighters were relayed in this pattern to attack the areas around Dover from as early as 0700 hours until mid morning. These were intercepted by a number of RAF fighter squadrons and casualties were suffered on both sides.

The action over southeast England then switched to a convoy (code named *Booty*) that had been identified further up the east coast near Harwich and Felixstowe. The Bf 110 fighter-bombers of *Erprobungsgruppe 210* had the range for this, but the 3rd *Staffel* aircraft did not, so the unit's twin-engine aircraft were escorted by Bf 110 fighters from ZG 26 *(Horst Wessel),* attacking the convoy around midday. Both of the *Zerstörer* units took losses off the east coast, with *Erprobungsgruppe 210* losing two aircraft off Harwich and ZG 26 also losing two in the same general area, with a further two returning to France damaged.

The German force was followed some two hours later by Dornier Do 17 bombers from KG 2, also escorted by the Bf 110s from ZG 26. The bombers all returned to France, but three were so badly damaged that they were written off and four others were also damaged. All of these Dorniers carried numerous crew members who were wounded, as well as some fatalities.

As the operations against convoy *Booty* were reaching their conclusion, *Luftflotte 2* directed another attack against a small convoy that had left the Thames docks and was proceeding into the Estuary. The attacking force was made up of over 20 Ju 87s from *Hauptmann* von Brauchitsch's IV / LG 1, together with other Stukas probably from II / StG 1, all with Bf 109 escorts. This group was intercepted around 1420 hours by Hurricanes from Croydon's 111 Squadron which lost five aircraft with four pilots killed.

Two Bf 109s from JG 3 and one from JG 51 were lost, with all three pilots killed or listed as missing. The Stukas appear to have returned to base without casualties. Despite the losses suffered by the Bf 109 escorts, the raiders pressed home an attack on a destroyer and two minesweepers, one of which suffered several casualties and was eventually beached under the North Foreland.

Two barrage balloons fall in flames over the Kent coast after attacks by Jagdwaffe fighters.

August – Adlertag
Eagle Day

12th August 1940

Over the Channel and southeast England, Monday dawned with fine weather and mist that burned off as the day progressed. The long range weather forecasts that had been passed to German High Command pointed to the following day, the 13th of August, bringing the fair conditions that would allow the *Adlertag* attacks to proceed.

The operational plan for the 12th of August shifted the target focus progressively inland and away from the Channel and coastal naval installations, aiming at airfields and their supporting infrastructure. The attacks were designed to move back and forth between the southeast and southwest sectors of the Channel in order to draw as many RAF fighters as possible into the conflict. The plan was doubtless to exhaust Fighter Command strength as much as possible in order to allow the following day's operations to proceed with weakened resistance.

The previous day's operations had also shown to German High Command something their intelligence arm had so far failed to appreciate fully. The series of high radio masts that could be seen around most of Britain's south and east coasts had to be contributing in some way to the RAF's ability to vector fighters to intercept the raids that the Luftwaffe sent over the Channel. It was decided to attack some of these sites in order to evaluate whether damage to these might reduce the *Luftwaffe* casualty rate as the intensity of the attacks increased.

There were various feints in the Dover area and offensive sweeps over Kent within a few hours of dawn. Two Spitfires from 610 Squadron were shot down over New Romney, and two others were damaged but returned to base. One pilot was burned and another wounded by the Bf 109s that caused the damage, but there were no fatalities. JG 26 was among those involved in these sweeps and *Oberleutnant* Friedrich Butterweck was killed when his 1st *Staffel* Bf 109 was shot down over Ashford, exploding at Elham at 0830 hours.

About half an hour later, *Erprobungsgruppe 210* mounted the first bombing attack of the day, aiming for the radar sites at Pevensey, Rye, Dover and Dunkirk (Canterbury). The 3rd *Staffel's* Bf 109s, led by Otto Hintze, went for the site at Dover, while Walter Rubensdörffer's Headquarters (*Stab*) flight attacked Canterbury, Martin Lutz's 1st *Staffel* headed for Pevensey and Wilhelm-Richard Rössiger's 2nd *Staffel* targeted Rye. Dover's facilities were hit by three bombs, but continued to operate on emergency equipment. The other three sites sustained sufficient damage to force them out of operation temporarily, but emergency equipment had the facilities back in operation later in the day, Rye by midday and both Dover and Pevensey by mid afternoon. The radar masts themselves at all of the sites remained standing, apparently undamaged.

Nevertheless, for a period on the 12th of August, the *Luftwaffe* had torn a vulnerable hole in Fighter Command's defence system. The raiders returned to France without suffering any casualties, mercifully unaware of the potential chaos they had caused. There was no immediate attempt to exploit the temporary loss of radar cover, as much through ignorance of the impact the raids had produced as for any other reason.

Dover was bombed after the raid on the radar sites and around 0930 hours the forward airfield at Lympne received the attentions of KG 2's Dornier Do 17s. Lympne had been used as a forward base by various groups of fighters within the Biggin Hill Sector, flying to the coast in the early morning to remain there throughout the day, before returning to their home bases in the evening. The Dorniers from KG 2 made a low approach to the airfield at 800 feet and dropped some 141 bombs in and around the field, putting it out of action for several days because of cratered landing areas and severed cabling.

Further west, *Luftflotte 3* was en route to Portsmouth and the Isle of Wight with 63 Junkers Ju 88 bombers from KG 51, escorted by close to 150 Messerschmitt Bf 110s and 109s. The bulk of the bombers hit the dockyards and Portsmouth itself, but the most telling damage was done to the all-important radar site at Ventnor on the Isle of Wight. This was badly damaged in the raid and remained out of action for three weeks. Despite this success, the *Luftwaffe* force suffered heavy casualties, but it was yet another potentially-damaging blow to Fighter Command's defence umbrella.

After midday, the action moved back to the Kent coast, where various airfields around the coastal strip were attacked. John Ellis was by this time leading 610 Squadron as Squadron Leader and his combat report for the 12th of August seems to suggest he was probably responsible for the loss of two Bf 109s that were shot down over New Romney that day. II / JG 52 lost both *Leutnant* Gehlaar and *Leutnant* Kern over the Kent coast.

> *I was leading 610 Sqdn which was detailed to intercept raid approaching Dungeness... In the dogfight I chased one solitary Me. 109 flying very fast and diving slightly. He rolled on to his back as I opened fire and I continued firing as he started his vertical dive, I could see my bullets entering the side of his fuselage as I followed him down. I broke off the attack as I was convinced he was diving out of control, he was also drawing away from me rapidly. F/O Lamb, who was behind me, later reported he saw this e/a continue its dive into the sea and break up.*

> *I climbed up again to 15,000 over Dungeness and spotted another Me 109 climbing into the sun. I caught him at about 20,000. He started to spin down to the left soon after I opened fire. I fired the remaining ammunition at very close range as he was spinning, but he presented an extremely difficult target. When I broke off the attack his engine was ticking over slowly and he was still spinning violently and he appeared to be out of control. Noticing a scrap going on just above I left the Me 109 and returned to re-arm.*

Around 1300 hours, *Erprobungsgruppe 210* returned to attack Manston with 14 Bf 110 fighter-bombers and seven Bf 109s. They had joined up over the French coast in a coordinated sortie with Bf 109 escorts from I /JG 26, III / JG 54 and 18 Dornier Do 17s from KG 2, the Dorniers attacking the airfield after the fighter-bombers had completed their low level bombing runs. The airfield was put out of action until the following day.

As *Erprobungsgruppe 210* withdrew to France, they were attacked by Spitfires from 54 Squadron and Hurricanes from 501 Squadron. These were reinforced by Spitfires from 65 Squadron that had earlier been taxiing out to take-off from Manston as the bombs began to fall. They were fortunate that the bombs dropped by the fighter-bombers had been directed more at the airfield's buildings, rather than the airstrip they were using, and all except one of these Spitfires succeeded in taking off to chase the *Luftwaffe* aircraft.

Among these was Vickers Supermarine's test pilot, Jeffrey Quill, who was on temporary attachment to 65 Squadron in order to assess the Spitfire's combat performance. As he raced to take off among the bomb explosions around the airfield, a Bf 109 passed across in front of him and he opened fire, slamming his throttle boost fully open to get maximum power. The German aircraft sped on and disappeared into cloud.

Returning from the Manston raid, *Leutnant* Erich Beudel, of *Erprobungsgruppe 210's* 1st *Staffel*, was attacked by a Hurricane which hit his Bf 110 in the radiators, despite which he was able to make it home with an overheated engine that finally seized as he landed. He'd probably been attacked by the Hurricane piloted by Flying Officer Kazimierz Lukaszewicz from 501 Squadron based at Gravesend, who was himself attacked from below by *Leutnant* Horst Marx flying a 3rd *Staffel* Bf 109. Other *Jagdwaffe* pilots may have also attacked the British aircraft which was lost in the sea off Margate, with Lukaszewicz posted missing. Beudel later recounted the experience.

Without any warning, numerous Spitfires and Hurricanes are on top of us. For the most part, we beat them off, then a Spitfire sits over me, ready to dive, but I was already in the saving clouds. I skipped from cloud to cloud over the Channel. Suddenly there are a few Hurricanes under the Bf 110s. From the left, one Hurricane gets underneath and behind me. My W/T operator shouts "Fighters!" and begins to loose off a drum. I close the radiator shutters tight and squeeze the last ounce out of the engines to catch up with a Kette which is only 100 metres in front of me.

The oil temperature goes over 110 degrees. Suddenly my W/T operator calls out "Tommy's down!" He had been followed by Leutnant Marx who got underneath him and gave him a burst. In the next second, he was snaffled by the 109 and fell blazing into the sea. Far below, a parachute opened. At last the coast is reached. The starboard engine's coolant and oil temperatures have risen to 120 degrees. Streams of blue smoke come from the engine, which must seize at any moment. Smoke fills the cockpit. I make an oblique landing and as I touch down the engine stops suddenly. All the coolant had run out owing to a single shot in the radiator, three glancing shots in the propeller and starboard wing.

Around 1700 hours, forewarned by the RDF plots and the Observer Corps. spotters high up on the ramparts of Dover Castle, 11 Group scrambled 610 Squadron from Biggin Hill and 501 Squadron from Gravesend to intercept an incoming force that had been forming up over the French coast. This was made up of 15 Junkers Ju 88s of II / KG 76 with an escort of Bf 109s from JG 54. As the German force approached the Kent coast, a furious dogfight took place between the bombers' escorts and the Spitfires and Hurricanes that were waiting.

The bombers split into two groups, one attacking Hawkinge and the other heading again for Lympne. Until then comparatively unscathed, Hawkinge airfield suffered heavy damage, with the workshops, two of the main hangars and the equipment stores damaged by bombs, with many others exploding all over the landing area. At Lympne, the second group dropped numerous bombs on the airfield and the surrounding fields, adding to the damage already inflicted earlier that day. The Hawkinge Operations Book record described the raid as follows.

Bombing attack by Ju 88's against the Station was carried out at 1730 hours and lasted approximately 10 minutes. One hangar, No. 3, was almost completely wrecked whilst one other, No. 5, was partially wrecked. A number of bombs of heavy calibre, including incendiary, were dropped. The aerodrome and buildings were machine-gunned during the attack. The main stores were partly damaged by fire, the clothing store almost completely. The fire was quickly brought under control by RAF personnel aided by local AFS. The Station Workshops were wrecked. Two houses in the Airmen's Married Quarters, occupied by airmen, were destroyed. Twenty-eight craters were made on the aerodrome, the longest being 76' x 72' x 28' deep and the smallest 10' x 10' x 8' deep, but the aerodrome was not rendered completely unserviceable. Repairs to the surface were immediately commenced by the RE's already attached for such work. Ground defences were surprised and no guns, except two Hispano, were fired. The altitude of the attacking aircraft was such that it was impracticable for the PACU to be brought into action. Two civilians employed by contractors of the Works Directorate were killed, and three airmen were killed. Six airmen received severe injuries and were admitted to the Kent and Canterbury Hospital, Canterbury. The Casualties occurred to personnel employed in No. 3 Hangar. Two Spitfire aircraft, under repair, were damaged, whilst one or two others were struck by splinters. Two non-operational aircraft on charge were damaged but repairable.

As this first raid on Hawkinge departed, some Hurricanes from 32 Squadron that had been patrolling the airspace needed to land and refuel. It soon became clear that there was more to come. While the Hurricanes were being refuelled, with the pilots helping the ground crews, the drone of more aircraft approaching caused everyone to look up. They all ran for cover when it became clear that the approaching aircraft were not friendly and more bombs began to explode across the field. *Erprobungsgruppe 210* had returned for its third and final sortie of the day, hitting Hawkinge shortly after 1730 hours and causing considerable further damage to the airfield. The German unit had managed a successful series of operations that day, with all aircraft returning safely, even though one, Beudel's, was damaged.

It was probably during the fighting that took place around the Hawkinge raid and the later sorties conducted by the *Luftwaffe* around 1730 hours that Pilot Officer Geoffery Page from North Weald's 56 Squadron was shot down and terribly burned. His squadron had been scrambled in an effort to find some German bombers that were detected inbound over the Kent coast. Page's Hurricane "Little Willie" was badly hit by German gunfire and Page baled out severely burned and with hands that were crippled by the burning fuel that had made his cockpit into an inferno. He was eventually picked up by a tender off Epple Bay near Margate, later transferred to the lifeboat.

At the entrance to the Capel-le-Fern Battle of Britain Memorial stands the replica of the Mark 1Hurricane flown by Geoffery Page when he was shot down with horrific burns on the 12th of August off the Kent coast around Margate.

Geoffery Page became one of the early "guinea pigs" of Sir Archibald McIndoe's ground-breaking burns unit at the Queen Victoria Hospital in East Grinstead, undergoing a long series of operations that were aimed at repairing his burned face and his crippled hands. Thanks to Page's fortitude and to no small degree to the skill of Archibald McIndoe, he eventually managed to rejoin the service in 1943 was able to fly operationally. He survived the war and remained a strong supporter of the East Grinstead hospital. In his later years he was instrumental in making possible the National Memorial to the Few from the Battle of Britain at Capel-le-Fern near Dover, fortunately surviving long enough to see the Museum opened by the late Queen Mother in 2000. He died later that year but his efforts to create and support the Museum were marked by the permanent location of a Mark 1 Hurricane replica, decorated as closely as possible to the way "Little Willie" looked before it was shot down over the Channel on the 12th of August 1940.

Oberleutnant Albrecht Dress was wounded in combat over the Channel coast during one of the late evening sorties on the 12th of August 1940, force landing his Messerschmitt Bf 109 E-4 at Hengrove near Margate. (Via Goss)

Several small raids on Kent coastal towns were undertaken during the evening as Kesserling tried to assess whether the early morning attacks against the Kent and Sussex radar facilities had depleted the effectiveness of Fighter Command's detection and warning system. The damage at Pevensey, Rye and Dover had already been repaired on a permanent or temporary basis by mid afternoon. As a result, the radio intercepts General Wolfgang Martini, the *Luftwaffe*'s signals chief, picked up following these evening sorties suggested that the attacks on the radar sites had not affected the way Fighter Command worked in detecting and intercepting incoming raids for more than a few hours. Further west, the continued inaction at the Ventnor site on the Isle of Wight was covered up by dummy signals as mobile radar units were moved in to fill the gap. Ventnor was out of action for three weeks, a development that would have been catastrophic if extended in a similar way throughout the southeast of Britain.

During a later post mortem on the first few days' attacks, this all served to support Göring's conclusion that attacks on the radar sites were a waste of time. This was a fortunate turn of events for Britain, since the continued operation of the radar umbrella remained the cornerstone of its aerial defence.

13th August 1940

As the ground crews of the *Luftwaffe* units assigned to the first attacks of *Adlertag* prepared their machines for the day's operations, the weather reconnaissance aircraft out over the Atlantic and the western approaches brought the news that cloud was building up and a delay would be advisable. Perhaps the pattern of good weather of the previous two days wasn't going to continue and another unsettled spell would delay the attacks still further. Göring issued orders to postpone the morning's missions, concerned that the threat of more bad weather could undermine his boasts of the coming day's success. He desperately wanted to avoid Hitler's disappointment and the inevitable displeasure this would produce.

With everyone poised and eager to launch the early morning sorties, orders for the postponement didn't get to everyone they should. As a result, despite the French coast still being covered with low cloud, bomber units from *Luftflotte 2* began to leave their bases to form their planned attack formations. *Luftflotte 2* headquarters in Brussels frantically signalled the order to delay departure until better weather conditions finally arrived. The mixed success in getting this through to some units was caused by a number of factors, whether this was through interference from atmospheric conditions, faulty equipment or ill-co-ordinated radio traffic remains to some extent unclear. The result was that *Luftflotte 2* was unable to recall most of the bomber unit undertaking the first of the day's raids and *Luftflotte 3* had similar problems with units involved in a second raid in the west, so laying the foundations for the chaos that Göring had hoped to avoid.

Shortly after dawn, III / JG 26 had taken off on an uneventful sweep over the Kent coast ahead of a scheduled attack on Eastchurch airfield planned by KG 2. *Oberst* Johannes Fink, the unit's *Kommodore*, had been given the honour of leading the first major attack of *Adlertag*, now that his role of *Kanakafü* (Channel Battle Leader) had been completed and the focus of attacks was moved inland to mainland Britain. Soon after 0500 hours, 80 of Fink's Do 17s rendezvoused over the cloudy French coast, anticipating the appearance of their escort of Bf 110s from ZG 26, before heading for their targets, the airfields at Sheerness and Eastchurch.

Somehow Fink and the bulk of his formation had failed to receive the recall order since most of the bombers had switched radio frequencies to allow communication between the various sections of the bomber formation, and this prevented them receiving the recall order. The Bf 110 escort from ZG 26 and some of Fink's own bombers from I / KG 2 did however receive the recall and turned back. Unable to contact Fink by radio, the Bf 110 escort commander, tried to warn him to turn back by wildly circling Fink's aircraft. He was another veteran of the First World War, *Oberstleutnant* Joachim Huth, a pilot somewhat akin to Douglas Bader, who overcame the loss of a leg to remain in front-line operations. Fink took Huth's aerobatics as a show of good spirits rather than anything more ominous. Bomber units usually operated on different radio frequencies to those used by the fighter squadrons, a curious practice that prevented bomber formations from talking directly to their fighter escorts. This seems to have remained an operational shortcoming throughout the Battle of Britain.

As the bulk of KG 2 continued, Fink concluded that his inability to see his escorts was a sign that the Bf 110s were sensibly keeping clear of the bombers in the thick cloud that still covered the Channel, a wise precaution to avoid potential collisions.

The formation eventually passed Sheerness still covered in cloud, but after turning back for France spotted Eastchurch some three miles away through a gap in the cloud base. Eastchurch was a Coastal Command airfield, occasionally used by Fighter Command as an emergency landing ground, rather than one of the Fighter Command sector stations on which the *Luftwaffe* should have been concentrating. Some blame for this lay in *Luftwaffe* reconnaissance from the previous day that had shown a build-up of fighters at Eastchurch. It was only a temporary change of use for the airfield. A detachment of Spitfires from 19 Squadron in 12 Group had been using the airfield as a forward base and 266 Squadron had arrived the day before, only staying for two days. The reconnaissance pictures taken on the 12th of August would have therefore shown Eastchurch heavily populated by fighters, qualifying it as a worthwhile target.

On the morning of the 13th of August, Fink must have felt he was back in the good old days over Poland and the Low Countries, when surprise attacks had caught the air forces of those countries with their aircraft on the ground, parked in long lines as if for inspection. A number of the units at Eastchurch that day had made the same mistake, making their aircraft tempting targets. This mistake was prevented at most British fighter bases, where aircraft were dispersed to perimeter E-shaped blast pens that prevented wholesale blast damage.

Scrambled earlier, 74 Squadron's Spitfires from Hornchurch found the Dorniers over Whitstable at about 0700 hours, surprised that there was no fighter escort. They had in fact chanced on the rear element of Fink's formation, while the front elements were already dropping their bomb loads on Eastchurch without opposition. Hurricanes from 111 and 151 Squadrons joined in as the Dorniers were returning home, shooting down five in total, with seven more bombers returning to France damaged, many with wounded on board.

In a curious postscript that came to light in late 2012 as a result of assiduous research by two aviation archaeologists including the well-respected Andy Saunders, two crew members from one of the Dorniers that had been shot down early that morning were finally accorded their appropriate funeral honours.

The bulk of KG 2's losses during this sortie were from the 7th *Staffel* which returned to base minus four of the bombers that had earlier taken off to attack the Kent airfields. Among these four, all of which were brought down at various locations on the north Kent coast, was the Dornier piloted by *Oberleutnant* Horst von der Gröben. His aircraft was brought down by British fighters on the shoreline near Whitstable, although it's unclear whether this was as a result of the attentions of the Hurricanes of 111 Squadron that seem to have shot down several of the other 7th *Staffel* aircraft. Von der Gröben was listed as missing although his body was later recovered from the sea, having been washed out of the remains of his bomber. One of the other crew members, *Oberleutnant* Gerhard Muller, was also recovered nearby. He'd managed to bale out of the doomed Dornier, but died when his parachute failed to open.

Both airmen were buried together in a Whitstable churchyard. However, confusion started when the same plot was later used to inter the remains of four other German airmen who had been recovered locally, these being placed in a single coffin on top of those of von der Gröben and Muller. After it was inaugurated in 1967, the beautiful site at Cannock Chase in Staffordshire, established by the British government and the German War Graves Commission, became the resting place for the German war dead that had initially been interred throughout the country, generally close to where they fell. However, while local records showed that Whitstable had been the final resting place for a total of 11 German airmen who died during this period, only nine individuals were actually recorded as having been re-interred in Staffordshire. Apparently, when the coffin containing the remains of the four other airmen buried on top of von der Gröben and Muller was moved, the bodies of these two earlier casualties were left behind, apparently forgotten. Belatedly, a comparison between the names recorded in Cannock Chase and locally in Whitstable pointed to the error and eventually the location of the forgotten resting place was discovered. After consultation with the German pilot's family, it was concluded that the bodies of these two unfortunate German airmen should be reunited with their colleagues at Cannock Chase.

The battles on the morning of the 13th of August 1940 were not all one-sided. Defensive fire from the ordered formations that the RAF fighters found over north Kent proved disturbingly effective. Before 0800 hours, one Spitfire from 74 Squadron was abandoned by its pilot, Flight Lieutenant Stanislav Brzezina, following an explosion in the cockpit caused by gunfire from the Dornier gunners. Brzezina baled out and the burning remains of his aircraft crashed into the Thames Estuary off the Kent coast. Two other Spitfires from this squadron were also damaged by the concentrated fire from the bombers, landing in one way or another to be repaired for later service. The KG 2 gunners also severely damaged three Hurricanes from 111 Squadron, but all of these managed to limp back to Croydon where they would be handed over to the repair squads. There were fortunately no pilot casualties from any of these losses.

On his return to France, Fink vented his anger over the absence of escorts and the botched recall order to a chastened and apologetic Kesserling.

It's possibly this bomber group's experiences during this sortie that fostered the growing unease among the bomber crews throughout the Battle of Britain when they were unable to see their fighter escorts close by. The *Jagdwaffe's* usual tactics used superior height and speed to manoeuvre into the sun and dive unexpectedly on any British fighters climbing to attack the bomber formations below. As the air assaults progressed however, there were frequent instances where bombers without close escort were being attacked from below while the escorting *Jagdwaffe* high cover was still manoeuvring for this tactical advantage far above. Typically, the fighters preferred to operate at around 25,000 feet or more, while the bombers usually approached their targets at between 15,000 and 18,000 feet. KG 2 on the Eastchurch raid, were operating at a significantly reduced height due to the cloud cover, probably bombing from less than 2,500 feet.

The wreckage of Dornier Do 17Z U5+DS from the 8th Staffel / KG 2 after crashing on mudflats at Seasalter during the Eastchurch raid on the 13th of August 1940. Only one of the four crew members survived the attack from the Hurricanes that brought the aircraft down.

It became an issue that continuously forced Göring to increase the number of fighters assigned as bomber escorts, as well as insisting that as many as one-third of the fighters should stay close to the bomber formations. Many of the German fighters were therefore forced increasingly to sacrifice their usual tactical height and speed advantages, factors that had often allowed them to cause heavy casualties among unsuspecting British fighters. This was to remain a sore subject for the men of the *Jagdwaffe*, who followed each variation of escort tactics dictated by Göring, generally achieving a good record in protecting the bombers, but at the same time almost always suffering heavily and rarely receiving the praise that their efforts may have deserved. For the *Luftwaffe's* commander, himself a decorated fighter pilot from the First World War, who you would expect to sympathise with his own fighter pilots' needs, it remains an aspect of this period of the war that I can't quite rationalise were it not perhaps partly caused by Göring's drug dependency.

Eastchurch nevertheless suffered a lot of damage with many casualties, and the airfield was out of operation until much later that day. Contemporary reports of the damage suggest several Spitfires and other aircraft were destroyed or damaged on the ground during this attack, but the casualty returns do not support this. One of 266 Squadron's Spitfires was damaged on the ground and five Coastal Command Blenheims were destroyed, but not quite the level of damage that the *Luftwaffe* had believed. In the eyes of *Luftwaffe* intelligence however, the airfield was written off as completely destroyed.

Lying on the Canterbury – Folkestone railway line near Barham in Kent, this Dornier Do 17 from Stab KG 2 had been shot down on the Eastchurch raid, losing one engine and making a force landing. (Via Goss)

Despite quite heavy casualties in KG 2 due to the lack of fighter escort, the raid's results must have been encouraging for the *Luftwaffe*. Fighter Command had been unable to get as many fighters into position as it might have wanted since cloud obscured the German formation's position, making it difficult for the Observer Corps. to clarify the radar intercepts. After raiders crossed the British coast, the RDF system was unable to help the sector controllers in Fighter Command since the radar facilities only covered the seaward approaches to Britain.

Luftflotte 2 was not the only air group to have failed to react to Göring's postponement of operations. In the west, *Luftflotte 3* mounted early morning sorties against two airfields in Hampshire and the naval facilities at Portland. Farnborough was targeted by 20 Junkers Ju 88s from I / KG 54, while 18 Ju 88s from II / KG 54 headed towards Odiham in northeast Hampshire. The former was the home of the Royal Aircraft Establishment, which mainly tested new aircraft types as well as evaluating captured aircraft, while Odiham was occupied by the Army Co-operation Corps., neither target offering much in the way of strategic influence on the strength of Fighter Command. Portland was to receive the attentions of a large force of Junkers Ju 87 Stukas from StG 77, but this force returned to base since the target area was obscured by cloud.

An escort comprising Bf 110s from *V (Zerstörer) / Lehrgeschwader 1* (V (Z) / LG 1) and Bf 109s from JG 2, JG 27 and JG 53 completed the mission package. Despite this, the Ju 88s were harried by RAF fighters, experiencing "strong and stubborn" fighter resistance from the moment they crossed the British coastline. Due to cloud and the attentions of the British fighters, the Ju 88s missed their targets and returned home having lost four bombers, with a further 11 being damaged to one degree or another.

It was *Luftflotte 3* that started off the afternoon's missions after the official go-ahead for the *Adlertag* operations was received from Göring. Both Ju 88s and Ju 87s were sent against a number of airfields in 10 Group in the southwest. The poor weather continued to hamper effective bombing of the original targets selected and some of the bombing force selected alternative targets such as Southampton. It was during this series of attacks that Spitfires from 609 Squadron found themselves the grateful recipients of the opportunity to attack an unescorted formation of Ju 87 Stukas. II / StG 2 lost six out of a formation of nine aircraft, together with their crews while their escort was embroiled in action with other RAF fighters.

Back in the southeast, after a comparatively quiet morning due to the cloudy conditions over the Channel and southeast England, *Erprobungsgruppe 210* took off from their advanced landing ground at Calais-Marck. They rendezvoused with an escort of Bf 110s from *Hauptmann* Wilhelm Makrocki's I / ZG 26 and flew across Channel at 11,000 feet, heading for Rochford airfield near Southend. Over Kent however, the cloud intervened again, forming a solid barrier at 3,700 feet which effectively prevented the fighter-bombers carrying out their planned attack. Turning back for home, *Erprobungsgruppe 210* released their bombs randomly over the Canterbury area, regaining the French coast without incident.

The escorting Bf 110s from ZG 26 were not quite so fortunate, with three of their aircraft either crashing or force landing on their return to France, with one gunner wounded. The pilot of a fourth aircraft, *Leutnant* Joachim Köpsell of the 1st *Staffel*, became so disorientated by the cloudy conditions on the return flight that he eventually crash-landed in Holland, some 165 miles from base. A fifth aircraft, flown by *Oberleutnant* Karl Fuchs of the 3rd *Staffel*, was shot down by a 56 Squadron Hurricane, possibly flown by Flying Officer Peter Weaver, exploding over Warden Bay on the Isle of Sheppey around 1500 hours. The crew was identified three days later only by shreds of clothing labels recovered from the aircraft's wreckage.

North Weald's 56 Squadron did not emerge unscathed from this engagement over the north Kent coast, losing three Hurricanes over the Sheppey/Sheerness/Faversham area to the retreating Bf 110s. All three pilots baled out, one unhurt and the two others injured. A fourth Hurricane was badly damaged and written off trying to make a force landing at Hawkinge, but the pilot escaped without injury.

Late in the afternoon, some 86 Ju 87s in two groups crossed the Kent coast at Dungeness and Dover, escorted by the whole of *Major* Gotthard Handrick's JG 26. *Hauptmann* Berndt von Brauchitsch's IV / LG 1 headed towards Detling airfield, while *Hauptmann* Anton Keil's II / StG 1 made for targets either in North Kent or across the Thames Estuary on the Essex coast, both units reinforced with Stukas from I / StG 1 moved up from western France for this sortie. It has been suggested that Keil was heading either for the Short Brothers aircraft factory at Rochester, Gravesend or even Rochford. Whatever the target, he was unable to find it due to navigational problems and cloud cover, and the retreating Stukas jettisoned their bombs over Canterbury and other parts of Kent when attacked by Hurricanes from 56 Squadron.

The results of the Detling raid were much more dramatic, with von Brauchitsch's 40 Stukas badly damaging another Coastal Command airfield, destroying 22 aircraft, buildings and causing many casualties, the dead including the Station Commander and 67 others. The Stukas had been allowed to bomb the airfield without any interference from British fighters, whose attention was taken up by a skirmish with II / JG 26, which had been operating ahead of and above the dive-bombers. In the variable visibility afforded by the cloudy conditions, the British fighters had been unable to spot the bombers because of a dense cloud bank between their position and Detling. With no losses, the Stuka formation returned to France, reprieved from the heavy casualties that the dive-bomber groups in the southwest had suffered at the hands of the jubilant RAF fighter pilots that came across their formations without fighter escort.

JG 26 lost one Bf 109 during this sortie, supposedly the victim of an attack from a Spitfire. The pilot was *Unteroffizier* Hans Wemhöner from the unit's 5th Staffel, whose aircraft crashed near Denton where he was taken prisoner around 1615 hours.

The first day's assault against the airfields meant that 11 Group's all-important fighter bases were afforded another reprieve, even though *Luftflotte 2* may have considered the damage to Eastchurch and Detling as positive steps towards the destruction of RAF Fighter Command. It was a mistake they frequently repeated, even though the message gradually got through as the month progressed and the focus turned more consistently towards Fighter Command's critically-important sector airfields such as Biggin Hill, Hornchurch and Kenley.

14th August 1940

The patchy weather continued, with occasional drizzle and a cloud base of some 2,000 feet which limited activity on any scale until midday when the conditions started to clear.

The usual morning reconnaissance missions had been carried out, one of which was tracked off the Kent coast and a flight of Hurricanes was sent to intercept the inquisitive Dornier Do 17. This was successful, but again the gunners in the German bomber demonstrated that they could be an effective deterrent for the unwary. One of the British fighters attacking the Dornier was damaged, crashing into the sea. The pilot baled out and was fortunate enough to be rescued.

Shortly before this, the Bf 110s from the 1st and 2nd *Staffeln* of *Erprobungsgruppe 210* took off from Denain to move to their forward base of Calais-Marck, the plan for the day's sortie being an attack on the airfields at Manston and Ramsgate. The latter was of no military significance, in reality being a small civilian airfield that wasn't used by the RAF, let alone by Fighter Command. After refuelling at Calais-Marck, the unit received the order to postpone departure due to the poor weather over the Channel and the Kent coast.

Returning home from attacks during the early part of the summer of 1940, this picture shows how the formations could bring heavy defensive fire against any British fighters attacking the formations of 3 or 5 aircraft close together. (Via Goss)

As the morning passed without significant activity, the cloud over the south coast began to break up and it wasn't long before the radar plots identified the beginnings of a formation gathering over Calais.

This was a large group Ju 87 Stukas from both II / StG 1 and IV / LG 1, escorted by all three *Gruppen* of JG 26, with further fighter protection provided by II / JG 52. The direction they followed initially confused the radar plotters, but finally the German aircraft settled on a course that pointed to targets around Dover and Folkestone. They were intercepted by four RAF squadrons from Biggin Hill, Kenley and Hornchurch, and a huge dogfight took place over Dover, involving as many as 200 aircraft. *Hauptmann* Kurt Fischer's I / JG 26 stayed to protect the Ju 87s, while *Hauptmann* Karl Ebbighausens's II *Gruppe* engaged the fighters. *Major* Adolf Galland's III *Gruppe* provided top cover in the form of an offensive sweep.

Despite the numbers of aircraft involved, it appears that all the Ju 87s managed to achieve was sinking the Goodwin Lightship, a curious strategic target, while the Bf 109s shot down seven of Dover's barrage balloons. LG 1 lost one Stuka into the waters of the Channel with the crew of *Oberleutnant* Kurt Gramling and his gunner, *Unteroffizier* Frans Scwatzki, declared missing. This casualty was attributed to an attack by Pilot Officer Keith Lofts of 615 Squadron, although it's possible that it was also hit during attacks by Spitfires from 610 Squadron, such was the confusion of the engagement. A second machine returned to France damaged with its gunner, *Unteroffizier* August Muller, wounded.

The *Jagdwaffe* meanwhile lost six Bf 109s early that afternoon, three from II / JG 52 on a sweep over Canterbury and two from JG 3, both of which crashed into the Channel off Dover. All the pilots are listed as killed or missing. The sixth Bf 109 was from the 1st *Staffel* of JG 26 and the pilot, *Feldwebel* Gerhard Kemen, was badly injured by machine gun fire from a 32 Squadron Hurricane. Kemen lost consciousness as he baled out of his stricken aircraft, waking up in Dover Hospital, a POW who was later destined to be repatriated back to Germany due to the severity of his injuries.

This action also left four Spitfires and three Hurricanes with varying degrees of battle damage, a further three Hurricanes being destroyed or written off. Two pilots from 615 Squadron were killed and a Spitfire pilot from 610 Squadron was injured force landing his damaged aircraft.

As the Stuka formation was crossing the Channel towards Kent, the Bf 110 fighter-bombers from *Erprobungsgruppe 210* took off, heading towards Kent escorted by Bf 109s, although two of the Bf 110s were forced to return to base due to mechanical problems. With the attention of the RAF fighters focussed on the Stukas, the remaining Bf 110s slipped along in their wake. The 1st *Staffel* was supposed to attack Ramsgate, but this was frustrated by barrage balloons over the harbour, so they joined up with the 2nd *Staffel* to attack vulnerable Manston once more. The formation had been tracked along the Kent coast by Fighter Command's sector control, probably concluding this was another fighter sweep, but the Manston defences were nonetheless alerted to the potential danger.

In addition to the 40 mm Bofors guns manned by Army crews, Manston's anti-aircraft defences consisted of various light automatic weapons operated by the air gunners of 600 Squadron's Blenheim night fighters. The base armoury had improvised a tripod-mounted battery of four Browning .303 inch machine guns which was located in an emplacement on top of the base rifle butts. An armoured car had also been modified with a mounting for a Vickers machine gun that allowed it to be used against attacking aircraft, and other improvised mountings equipped with 20 mm Hispano cannon were placed at various locations around the airfield. Forewarned of the raid's approach by sector control, on this occasion the gunners were waiting for the attack, manning what was a formidable anti-aircraft defence, particularly against low level attacks.

Hauptmann Walter Rubensdörffer's hard-working crews swept out of the haze low across the airfield. They dropped their 500 kg bombs, destroying a hangar along with the three Blenheims from 600 Squadron it contained and providing a new collection of craters for the airfield personnel to fill in. This time however, the raiders would not all return safely to France as they had managed to do on previous missions – two aircraft being brought down over Manston by the ground defences.

As the fighter-bombers began to pull out of their bombing run over the airfield, one of the casualties was a Bf 110 from the 2nd *Staffel*, flown by *Leutnant* Heinrich Brinkmann with his gunner *Unteroffizier* Richard Mayer. It was hit by machine gun fire from 600 Squadron's air gunners and rolled into the ground, killing both crewmen, although there has been some suggestion that this aircraft was a casualty of collateral damage from the explosion that brought down the second Bf 110 that was lost.

The mangled wreckage of Hans Steding's Messerschmitte Bf 110 D after the raid by Erprobungsgruppe 210 on the 14th of August 1940.

Almost simultaneously, a second aircraft flown by *Unteroffizier* Hans Steding was hit by a 40 mm round from one of the Bofors guns and the tail section just aft of the gunner's position disintegrated, sending the remains of the forward fuselage tumbling to the ground. Arguably, the Bofors round had hit the oxygen bottles stored in the aft of the fuselage behind the gunner's position. As the two parts of the fuselage split apart, the aircraft's gunner, *Gefreiter* Ewald Schank, was dragged from his seat in the wake of the doomed machine. Almost miraculously, despite one of his boots being trapped in the rear cockpit, he managed both to free his foot from the boot and deploy his parachute in sufficient time to break his fall. He landed dazed but otherwise only superficially hurt and was dragged into a shelter by airfield personnel. After recognising his amazing escape, Schank fainted while his colleagues' bombs of were still exploding around the airfield, but later he regained consciousness in Manston's sick bay.

15th August 1940

Thursday morning dawned to reveal continued cloud and the same unsettled conditions that had already dislocated earlier German attacks against southern England. With few operations expected because of this, Göring convened a meeting of his senior commanders, Sperrle, Kesselring and Lörzer, at *Karinhall*, his luxurious mansion outside Berlin. The purpose of this meeting was to conduct a post mortem on the attacks of the preceding few days and decide how to adjust tactics to improve the results.

While they were thus engaged, the weather in the Channel cleared. *Oberst* Paul Deichmann, Chief of Staff of *Luftflotte 2* and Kesselring's deputy, emerged from the operations centre on the cliffs near Cap Blanc Nez to see that the weather had settled and the sun was shining. It was perfect for the sort of all-out assaults which had been planned earlier in August, ready to be implemented when the weather conditions allowed. He lost no time in setting things in motion, and gave the orders that started the day's orchestrated series of sorties. In addition to sending his own units off on their various missions, this was also the signal for *Luftflotte 3* in the west and *Luftflotte 5* from Scandinavia to perform their supporting roles.

Approaching midday, a large force of Ju 87s (12 dive-bombers from IV / LG 1 and 24 from II / StG 1 attacked the airfields at Hawkinge and Lympne respectively, protected by a strong fighter contingent from JG 51, JG 53, JG 54 and JG 26. Spitfires from 54 Squadron and Hurricanes from 501 squadron were sent to intercept them and apart from one Stuka that was shot down into the sea and a second that crashed around Folkestone, the *Jagdwaffe* appear to have been doing the job that was expected of them. There were no known Bf 109 casualties from this sortie although Fighter Command suffered several losses. 501 Squadron lost two Hurricanes destroyed and one damaged, while 54 Squadron lost three Spitfires with all three pilots injured to one degree or another.

Both Lympne and Hawkinge were damaged, the former so badly that it played only a minor role throughout the remainder of the Battle of Britain. Lympne was in any case not an operational fighter base, being used occasionally as a landing ground for fighter aircraft. However, the most dangerous effect of the raids on these two Kent airfields was something of a fluke. Many of the bombs intended for Hawkinge missed the target and struck the road outside the perimeter, with the German pilots perhaps distracted by heavy anti-aircraft fire from the airfield's defences as well as by nearby

British fighters. They severed the power cables in the road and, at a stroke, the power for the radar sites at Rye, Foreness and Dover were cut off, creating a gap in the south's radar screen that was not repaired until the end of the day.

At this point, while the defenders' attention was concentrated on the southeast, several attacks were launched by *Luftflotte 5* against targets in the north and northeast. These had limited success, but the losses incurred both to the German bombers and heavy fighters made it inadvisable to repeat similar sorties from Scandinavia in daylight.

This was the first and only occasion when *Luftflotte 5's* bombers would attempt to bomb the British coast in daylight from Scandinavia. The involvement of these units was based on the theory that Fighter Command had been stripping the fighter squadrons normally based in the northern counties to reinforce what *Luftwaffe* intelligence analysts thought were seriously depleted squadrons in the south. This should have meant that the industrial and military targets in the north of England would be defended by an almost token force as the attacks against southern England gathered pace.

Since the north of England was outside the range of Bf 109 escorts, the bomber forces assigned to the attacks were escorted mainly by Bf 110 fighters from I / ZG 76, equipped with huge and ungainly wooden belly fairings, housing additional fuel and oil tanks to extend their operational range – the Bf 110 D *Dackelbauch*. With this fuel tank containing some 230 gallons of extra fuel, this gave the twin-engine fighter more range but, at the same time, a significant weight and manoeuvrability handicap, made worse because the tanks and their fairings could not be jettisoned. One of the bomber groups flying Ju 88 bombers was also escorted by Ju 88 C heavy fighters.

They were all in for an unpleasant surprise and when the Hurricanes and Spitfires from 13 and 12 Group rose to intercept the approaching radar plots from Scandinavia, they learnt two valuable lessons. Firstly, the north of England was still heavily defended by modern single seat fighters, as well as by the expected ground defences. Secondly, the day's results made it clear that the Bf 110 *Dackelbauch* was not the machine to engage in dogfighting with Spitfires and Hurricanes.

The day's operations had been planned with a view to swamping the British defence capability from Land's End to Scotland with a series of raids that would leave Fighter Command drowning in a tidal wave of successive raids that it would be unable to counter. Instead, out of a force of some 154 aircraft sent from *Luftflotte 5*, as many as 20 aircraft were lost, with numerous others returning to base damaged. *Luftflotte 5* limited itself from this point to maritime operations in the North Sea and night-time bombing sorties.

While these attacks were in progress around midday, Manston once more suffered from its exposed position on the northeast extremity of Kent when it was strafed by 12 Bf 109s. A Spitfire from 266 Squadron was damaged by cannon and machine gun fire during this attack.

Flight Lieutenant Al Deere of 54 Squadron had another narrow escape. At 20,000 feet over Dungeness, he and his colleagues were tracking one of the approaching German formations when a lone Bf 109 broke away and headed back towards France, possibly with mechanical problems. Deere broke away in pursuit and, keeping his aircraft in the pilot's blind spot, slightly below and behind the German fighter's tail plane, he gradually caught up as they both crossed the Channel. They passed through some cloud at 5,000 feet and as they emerged into clear sky again, Deere realised that he'd been concentrating so much on staying unseen and closing the range that he was now over France and close to Calais where so many of the *Jagdwaffe* units were based.

Even though he was still out of effective range, Deere let loose a burst of machine gun fire at the German aircraft which promptly dived for the ground as a number of other Bf 109s headed his way to teach this bold New Zealander a lesson. Deere turned back for Dover at full boost. Nevertheless, two German fighters came within range, hitting his Spitfire despite violent evasive manoeuvres. Finally, his aircraft was hit in the cockpit and engine, the incoming fire grazing his left wrist and sending spouts of black oil over his cowling. Over Ashford, with fire beginning to lick back from the engine compartment, it was time for him to part company from his doomed Spitfire, and he baled out. As his aircraft exploded in woodland below, he floated gently down nearby to the comparative safety of the Kent countryside.

Flight Lieutenant Al Deere, the New Zealand pilot that was in the thick of the action over southeast England during the summer of 1940 and had numerous close escapes leading to him being described as having nine lives.

‌‌

Three hours later, a formation tagged "Raid 22" by 11 Group's controllers attacked Martlesham Heath near Ipswich, damaging both the airfield and a signals station to the west of the airfield. It was *Erprobungsgruppe 210* again. They attacked the airfield while some Stukas that also formed part of the raid hit the nearby signals station. The entire German force returned to France without opposition.

While this was in progress in Suffolk, Rochester and Eastchurch airfields were attacked by 88 Do 17s from KG 3, escorted by 130 Bf 109s from JG 51, JG 52 and JG 54. In order to disguise their target, the bombers flew a dog-leg course on their approach, crossing the coast at Deal. As seven mixed Hurricane and Spitfire squadrons were scrambled to intercept the attack, more than 60 Bf 109s from JG 26 on an offensive sweep passed near Dover. The German bomber force was quite successfully protected by this huge fighter screen. KG 3 nevertheless lost two Do 17s over Kent and off the Kent coast during this raid, with a further six aircraft regaining the safety of the north French coast with varying degrees of damage and numerous crew members wounded. The escorting Bf 109s from both JG 51 and JG 54 also suffered with five aircraft lost or written off, and one damaged by the time it returned to France. Three pilots were either killed or missing and one had been rescued by Margate's lifeboat when his aircraft crashed into the sea nearby.

There was considerable damage at Rochester, where production of the RAF's first heavy bomber, the Short Stirling, was interrupted, and several completed aircraft were destroyed by the aircraft from II / KG 3. At Eastchurch, the repairs that had been necessary as a result of KG 2's raid on the 13th of August were put back by further damage from the bombs dropped by III / KG 3.

Three Hurricanes were damaged during the engagements surrounding these attacks, two from Croydon's 111 Squadron, with 64 Squadron losing two Spitfires and suffering damage to a third machine. One of the Spitfires lost was piloted by Pilot Officer Ralph Roberts who, according to German accounts, must have become disoriented, much as Al Deere had been earlier. Roberts was finally shot down close to the French airfield of Calais-Marck. He was interned as a POW after force landing in a sugar beet field near Calais, shot down by *Leutnant* Gerhard Müller-Dühe of the 7th *Staffel* / JG 26. He was the sixth claim by the German pilot, who was himself shot down and killed over Canterbury three days later. The pilot of the other Spitfire lost was posted as missing, the assumption being that his aircraft fell into the Channel and he drowned.

It was incidents like these that reinforced Dowding's increasingly pointed instructions to his Group Commanders and controllers that German raiders retreating to France should not be pursued beyond easy gliding distance of the British coast. However, the thrill of the chase and concentration on completing the "kill" would continue to lead British fighter pilots into exposed situations over the Channel itself, as well as occasionally over France.

Around 1700 hours, *Luftflotte 3* sent as many as 250 aircraft in a feint move towards the Isle of Wight, spreading out to hit a number of targets over Hampshire and Wiltshire. The airfield at Middle Wallop was dive-bombed by Ju 88s with Bf 110 escorts, while other objectives such as Worthy Down, Portland and Andover were also targeted. As many as 11 RAF fighter squadrons were vectored to intercept this huge mass of raiders and heavy casualties were inflicted, with the Bf 110 escorts suffering particularly badly.

As this raid was withdrawing and most of Keith Park's squadrons were in the process of rearming and re-fuelling, another group of *Luftwaffe* bombers and fighters was gathering over Calais. Despite being denied the use of the squadrons that had only recently landed, Park sent four squadrons from the eastern part of his group area to intercept this late afternoon raid. The German raiders were planning to make high level bombing runs over Biggin Hill and Kenley, but missed these primary targets, and identified West Malling as a suitable alternative. Yet to become an operational fighter base, the airfield suffered some damage and two airmen were killed by flying splinters.

Unteroffizier Balthasar Aretz stands in front of a new Messerschmitt Bf 110 D fighter-bomber on charge with the 2nd Staffel of Erprobungsgruppe 201 while mechanics check out the machine. (Via Goss)

It fell to the busy fighter-bombers of *Erprobungsgruppe 210* to make the final daylight strike of the day. All three *Staffeln* had left Calais-Marck in the early evening, bombed-up for another sortie, and they met up with their escort from JG 52 to launch the same sort of dive-bombing attack that had been so successful previously at Manston and Martlesham Heath. This time, the primary target was Kenley on the southern outskirts of

London. As the sun fell in the west, making visibility difficult in the evening haze, the JG 52 escort either ran short of fuel or decided the visibility was making the job of continuing the escort mission too dangerous and turned for home. *Gruppenkommandeur Hauptmann* Walter Rubensdörffer's Bf 110s and Bf 109s were by this time close to where they expected their target to appear and the sight of British fighters already close by made their situation particularly exposed.

Flying westwards into the setting sun with an early evening ground haze probably confused Walter Rubensdörffer's geographical confidence. *Oberleutnant* Otto Hintze, the 3rd *Staffel's* leader, reported hearing Rubensdörffer asking quizzically

Are we over land or sea? I'm going down.

To answer the question he had decided to lose height just as the group were passing over Croydon, Kenley's satellite airfield, slightly north and west of Kenley.

Perhaps misidentifying Croydon as Kenley, as well as getting concerned about the approaching British fighters, Rubensdörffer controversially decided to attack Croydon, inside the Greater London area and surrounded by residential property. Such attacks had been banned by Adolf Hitler and were only to be mounted with his sole authorisation, since he hoped to resolve the conflict with Britain without the need to invade even at this comparative late stage. Avoiding civilian casualties in "terror raids" was still part of this philosophy. There was significant damage to the airfield and factories surrounding it, as well as collateral damage and civilian casualties among the nearby houses.

Rubensdörffer's men also suffered heavy losses as they withdrew across Kent and Sussex, with Hurricanes from 111 Squadron based at Croydon and 32 Squadron from Biggin Hill, as well as 501 Squadron from Gravesend taking their toll of the Bf 110 fighter-bombers. Of the 22 aircraft from the group that bombed Croydon, seven Bf 110s and one Bf 109 were shot down over the Home Counties and one returned to Calais-Marck damaged from this raid. Most of those counted as destroyed fell in various parts of Surrey and Sussex, including Rubensdörffer's own aircraft, which was finally finished off over Rotherfield, not far from the Kent/Sussex border. It's believed that it was Pilot Officer "Ron" Duckenfield from 501 Squadron who administered the *coup de grâce* on the *Gruppenkommandeur's* Bf 110. However, two of the unit's aircraft came down in Kent.

Flight Lieutenant Michael Crossley was leading 32 Squadron's Red Section in an attack on one of the Bf 110s escaping from Croydon.

> *I attacked a Do 17 (sic) from astern and opened fire from 200 yards, setting the port engine on fire. I broke away and Red 2 closed in and knocked some pieces off it. He then gave way to Red 3 who also hit it. We followed and the fire appeared to go out, giving place to two streams of white. Red 2 and Red 3 went in and knocked it about so badly that it crashed east of Sevenoaks, the pilot escaping by parachute.*

This 2nd *Staffel* aircraft, crashed at Ightham, east of Sevenoaks, at 1700 hours and the pilot, *Leutnant* Helmut Ortner, managed to bale out safely, subsequently being detained by the Biggin Hill Military Police before being passed on to the usual POW interrogation centre at Cockfosters in London. Ortner's gunner, *Obergefreiter* Bernhard Lohmann, had been killed by the machine gun fire from the three Hurricanes from 32 Squadron.

The second Bf 110 that came down a few minutes later was flown by *Oberleutnant* Alfred Habisch, the gunner's position being occupied by *Unteroffizier* Ernst Elfner, who later recounted the tale of their demise.

> *After leaving the defence circle (abwehrkreis) we flew south alone at low*
> *altitude without any contact with fighters or AA (in the defence circle we*
> *had been hit by gunfire). Suddenly, the aircraft began to shake violently.*
> *After that it became difficult to control, so we came down at Hawkhurst.*
> *I was slightly wounded in the right hand by a bullet. We were encircled*
> *by the Home Guard. Then I was brought to a big barbed wire fence. I*
> *thought it was prepared for prisoners, waiting for the invasion, but I was*
> *the only one that sat in it while the sun was setting. I was eventually*
> *brought to Oldham. On the passage to Canada, on the ship "Duchess of*
> *York", I saw Habisch (his pilot), Koch (the unit's Adjutant who force*
> *landed near Eastbourne) and Ortner.*

Their 2nd *Staffel* Bf 110 D had suffered comparatively minor damage in the force landing near Hawkhurst and was put on display at Hendon Park later that month, before being shipped over to the United States for evaluation. Many of the detailed photographs of this variant of the Bf 110 that are in circulation today come from the aircraft's detailed examination by the Vultee Aircraft Corporation at Vultee, near Los Angeles in California.

There are no records of any losses among the Hurricanes that caused such a high level of casualties among the Bf 110s of *Erpobungsgruppe 210* that evening. With the escort from JG 52 long gone, the eight Bf 109 *Jabos* of the 3rd *Staffel* were the heavy fighters' principal defence against the marauding groups of Hurricanes, apart from the usually effective fire from the single machine gun in the rear gunner's position in each of the Bf 110s. On this occasion it appears that the Hurricanes managed to remain unaffected by either of these, the engagement being almost entirely one-sided. None of the surviving British combat reports covering this period talk of avoiding defensive fire from the rear cockpits of the aircraft they attacked. The gunners in at least three of the German casualties were either dead by the time the aircraft finally dived into the ground (e.g. Rubensdörffer's own aircraft and Ortners' Bf 110 that crashed at Ightham) or, as in the case of Koch's aircraft that force landed outside Eastbourne, the gunner was seriously injured. One of the Bf 109s from the 3rd *Staffel* that tried to come to Rubensdörffer's aid in his escape was also shot down over Frant in Sussex, the remaining seven Bf 109s returning to base, probably at the extreme limit of their fuel endurance

Alfred Habish's Messerschmitt Bf 110 D fighter-bomber is lifted from the trailer that transported the damaged aircraft from near Hawkhurst to Hendon where the aircraft was put on display.

It had been a trying day for all concerned in a variety of daylight sorties over Britain, but it was particularly bad for the *Luftwaffe*. Despite higher claims by the RAF at the time, the German raids had resulted in 76 *Luftwaffe* aircraft being lost with 128 airmen killed and others taken prisoner. Almost half of the aircraft lost were either Bf 109 or Bf 110 fighters, with their aircrew accounting for almost one-third of the airmen killed. Against this, Fighter Command lost 35 fighters, with 11 pilots killed. Little wonder it was remembered in the *Luftwaffe* as *der Schwarze Donnerstag* (Black Thursday), since the German losses on the 15th of August were the highest of any single day during the 1940 attacks on Britain.

16th August 1940

During the early morning, the Channel was slightly overcast and hazy. This cleared as the morning progressed to give fine conditions and high temperatures with some cloud building up later in the day.

After the hectic raids of the previous day, the morning passed with comparatively little activity showing up on the radar screens. It was not until midday that things began to change, giving the personnel of most RAF units some rest during a relatively quiet morning. A large German formation soon crossed the coast around Dungeness, this being made up of bombers from KG 2 and KG 76 with a strong fighter escort from JG 3, JG 51 and JG 54. The two bomber groups split up over the Thames Estuary, with KG 76 heading towards Biggin Hill and Kenley, while KG 2 made for Hornchurch, north of the Thames.

Despite the sector controllers' attention being drawn to the simultaneous approach of a second force approaching east of the Isle of Wight, 11 Group scrambled Hurricanes from 32 Squadron at Biggin Hill and 111 Squadron from Croydon, together with Spitfires from 266 Squadron at Hornchurch. The three squadrons headed directly for the bombers and a desperate, confused fight followed.

Flight Lieutenant Henry Ferriss from 111 Squadron demonstrated the potentially-fatal consequences of attacking bombers head-on, a tactic that his squadron had earlier adopted after it had been shown how effective this could be in breaking up the tight German bomber formations. He probably misjudged the timing of the last-minute break-off, easily done when the closing speed of the two opponents is around 500 mph. The effective range of the Hurricane's machine guns was less than 300 yards, so there was little time for more than 1-2 seconds of fire before the need to break away and avoid collision. The Hurricane's eight Browning machine guns put out a total of 160 rounds per second, but the bombers could normally take a lot of punishment before suffering fatal damage from the standard attack from behind since the crew compartment was protected by an armoured bulkhead. The same was not true in the case of an attack from the front.

Ferriss didn't judge it quite right, and his Hurricane collided over Marden with the Dornier Do 17 Z of *Oberfeldwebel* Wachter of the 7th *Staffel* / KG 76, killing himself and the German crew. His Hurricane crashed at Sheepshurdt Farm and the Do 17 came down near Paddock Wood at around 1245 hours.

The Dornier force moving towards Hornchurch also took casualties as they passed over Kent on the way back to France. One was shot down over Canterbury, with a second crashing in the waters of the Thames Estuary off the north Kent coast, both crews listed as killed or missing. A third Do 17 from the 3rd *Staffel* / KG 2 limped back to north France with damage sustained over Kent, finally crashing near Calais after being abandoned by its crew, who baled out with two wounded.

Throughout these attacks, *Jagdwaffe* groups were operating on offensive sweeps over Kent and the Home Counties. One of these was made up of the *Stab* (Headquarters) Flight of II / JG 26, led by their *Gruppenkommandeur*, *Hauptmann* Karl Ebbighausen, who was accompanied by four other pilots, including *Leutnant* Eckardt Roch, Waldi Maerz and Karl Borris. Ebbighausen was by this time one of the rising stars of the *Jagdwaffe*, with a tally of seven victories.

Soon after midday, they were bounced by seven Spitfires from 266 Squadron based at Hornchurch. This squadron had been transferred into No. 11 Group only a week earlier, during which time they had already lost three pilots. Despite bouncing the *Stabschwarm* of II /JG 26, it appears that they still had much to learn in terms of the battle awareness required to survive in the hectic southeast that summer.

As they dived on Ebbighausen's formation, they failed to check carefully enough above and behind and were in turn bounced by more Bf 109s from above. Joined by this second group of Bf 109s, the German pilots succeeded in dominating the engagement, and 266 Squadron finished up with five aircraft lost, one damaged, three pilots killed and two wounded. One of the pilots repeated the mistake made by others earlier, pursuing the retreating Bf 109s as they returned home low on fuel. Sub Lieutenant Henry La Fone Greenshields paid the price for this when he was shot down and killed by Bf 109s over Calais, crashing into a canal bank in the town's suburbs and burning out. He was probably shot down by *Leutnant* Walter Blume of the 7th *Staffel*. Soon after this, 266 Squadron was moved from Hornchurch back to Wittering in Leicestershire in No. 12 Group to recover from these losses.

Ebbighausen became the only recorded German casualty of this action, his aircraft crashing into the sea, curiously unseen by his colleagues. Karl Borris remarked on the encounter in his combat report.

> *Combat with seven Spitfires against five of us in the Stabschwarm. I hang at 7,000 metres behind our commander and Eckardt Roch, and behind us Liebing and Maerz. We were attacked from above and to the left by seven Spitfires. Dogfight. A 109 reacts by breaking swiftly away. It was Waldi Maerz. I could not warn him by radio because the equipment was not functioning. Maerz landed with 20 hits in his aircraft and a badly overheated engine. I can confirm a victory by Eckardt Roch..... From this flight, our commander, Hauptmann Ebbighausen did not return.*

Karl Ebbighausen became another of the experienced leaders that Göring was increasingly conscious of losing. He was not the only senior *Jagdwaffe* pilot to suffer that day. Among the other pilots shot down in the Channel was *Hauptmann* Alfred Müller, the *Staffelkapitän* of the 4th *Staffel* / JG 3, who was wounded but rescued from the sea by the *Seenotflugkommando*.

In the Dover Straits and the southeast, there followed a lull in operations, but the focus shifted to the west where Tangmere was heavily bombed and both Southampton and Portsmouth received the attentions of *Luftflotte 3*.

It was during the attacks on Southampton that one of the Hurricane pilots from 249 Squadron, then based at Boscombe Down in 10 Group, performed with gallantry that resulted in the only Victoria Cross awarded to a fighter pilot during the Second World War. The pilot was Flight Lieutenant James Nicholson, whose aircraft was bounced along with two colleagues as they climbed through 17,000 feet to rejoin the rest of their squadron after investigating some suspicious aircraft that turned out to be Spitfires.

All three aircraft were hit by Bf 110 twin-engine fighters, and Nicholson's Hurricane burst into flame. Despite this, he stayed in his cockpit long enough to fire at one of the Bf 110s that overshot. Eventually baling out, burned and wounded, he suffered the ultimate indignity of being wounded again as he came down when a Home Guard Sergeant let fly at him with a shotgun, mistaking him for a German pilot.

Back in the southeast, the afternoon saw a raid of over 100 aircraft approaching Dover at 1630 hours and a little later, another force of some 70 aircraft was plotted between the Isle of Sheppey and Hornchurch en route towards Debden. This group flew back down the Thames Estuary at 1730 hours and returned to France. These had simply been fighter sweeps which continued into the evening over Kent and the southeast's coast. At 1800 hours, some 16 Bf 109s from the 2nd and 3rd *Staffeln* of JG 52 under *Oberleutnant* Wolfgang Ewald strafed Manston, destroying a 65 Squadron Spitfire, a 600 Squadron Blenheim and damaging another.

As they approached the Manston area, Ewald had spotted various RAF fighters preparing to land at the airfield, refuel and re-arm. He ordered his formation to slow down and form line astern as if they were another group of fighters following the same approach pattern. Allowed in this way within a few hundred metres of the airfield without opposition, Ewald ordered his men to spread out and open fire, which they did with devastating effect. They escaped without loss.

From operations over Kent during the day, the *Luftwaffe* lost seven fighters and a further four Do 17s either destroyed or written off. In terms of personnel from these aircraft, six pilots and five NCOs were killed, one pilot taken POW, while five other airmen were wounded. Between 1830 and 1920 hours, enemy patrols were active between Cherbourg and the Straits of Dover, searching for the crews of the aircraft that had ditched in the Channel.

RAF casualties in the area totalled 13 aircraft lost and a further eight damaged, the bulk of the aircraft lost being the Spitfires from 266 Squadron. The pilot losses for the conflict had started to escalate, with seven killed and seven wounded from operations over Kent and the Dover Straits on the 16th of August. This had become a regular and debilitating pattern since the first attacks of the 13th of August, when the units operating over Kent managed to emerge with more limited casualties. Worse was to come later in the month.

18th August 1940

Saturday the 17th of August saw fine weather in the Channel area with hazy conditions further up the east coast of Britain. Despite the good weather, there was little activity in the skies over the Home Counties, most incursions made by *Luftwaffe* aircraft during daylight being primarily for reconnaissance purposes. Undoubtedly, these would have been in preparation for the intense series of raids being planned for the following day. On both sides of the Channel Sunday the 18th of August was dubbed "The Hardest Day", since both British and German forces suffered heavy losses from the intensive attacks carried out.

Sunday promised fine, warm temperatures with clear blue skies. Despite this, the weather patterns again proved frustrating for the *Luftwaffe* fliers as local conditions over their selected target areas delayed or prevented the execution of their planned operations. The morning saw a haze over the southeast of Britain, caused by temperature inversion that dispersed as the day progressed, but the afternoon brought cloud moving southeast from the midlands and the northwest.

Arguably, the mission planning staff at *Luftflotte 2* had finally come to realise which targets within 11 Group were the most critical and where damage would have a fundamental effect on Fighter Command's ability to put up the same punishing aerial defence that they had managed over the preceding week. All four of the main sector airfields around the outskirts of London, Kenley in Surrey, Biggin Hill in Kent, together with Hornchurch and North Weald in Essex were selected as targets for large groups of bombers with strong fighter escorts from both Bf 109 and Bf 110 units. The *Luftwaffe* planners didn't get it right all the time though, since airfields which had no connection to Fighter Command's operations continued to be attacked throughout August and early September, arguably a waste of valuable resources that could have been better employed focusing on 11 Group's sector airfields.

Although the *OKL* remained unaware of how important these were in controlling the daily sorties of the RAF fighter squadrons within their particular sectors, wholesale destruction of the all-important control rooms at these locations would have had serious implications. Had these four sector control rooms been put out of action or destroyed simultaneously, Fighter Command would have struggled to develop an alternative way of using the input from radar plots and Observer Corps. reports to bring the fighters into contact with incoming raids. Fortunately, it appears that the selection of these airfields was based on simpler assumptions. All four airfields were clearly large and established fighter bases that were used by several fighter squadrons as their home base. "Beppo" Schmid and his colleagues in *Luftwaffe* intelligence remained blissfully unaware of the sector control rooms' more critical importance.

For the *Luftflotte 2* units preparing for their missions against the southeast, the initial plans called for an early morning start. Sixty Heinkel He 111 bombers from KG 1 based around Amiens were to drop their bombs from high level on Biggin Hill. Kenley was to receive a complicated series of attacks by different *Gruppen* from KG 76, combining an initial attack by Junkers Ju 88 dive-bombers, followed by the unit's Dornier Do 17s dropping their loads from high level. The final strike by KG 76 was to have been from the specialist low level experts of the 9th *Staffel*, who would finish off the airfield's destruction.

The two airfields in Essex would be attacked later in the day, with KG 3's Heinkels targeting North Weald and KG 2's Dorniers heading for Hornchurch. All of the *Lufflotte 2* forces would be covered by heavy fighter escort from Bf 109s and Bf 110s from a mixture of different *Jagdwaffe* units, operating on offensive sweeps ahead of the bombers, alongside the bombers as direct (close) escort, and above the bomber formations as high-level escort. While the Essex airfield raids may seem to have little direct impact on life in the Kent countryside, a large part of the forces used on the 18th of August on these raids, as well as the Kenley attackers, either flew over Kent en route to their targets, or used the direct route across Kent to reach the coast and the safety of their French bases. This was not a feature unique to this day's activities and was one of main the reasons why 11 Group often placed its first line of defence between Canterbury and Maidstone, or between Canterbury and the coast at Margate.

While the civilian population of Kent and the south of England went about their Sunday routine with a fine, warm and sunny day in prospect, *Luftlotte 2's* plans began to go awry as KG 1 took off early in the morning to begin their approach to bomb Biggin Hill. As they manoeuvred into their formations for the cross-Channel flight, they were recalled to base since the haze over the target obscured visibility below 4,000 feet, preventing accurate bombing. These conditions were expected to change as the temperature rose and ground level visibility improved, so this mission and that of KG 76 was postponed for two and a half hours. Some two hours later, updated reconnaissance reports confirmed that low level visibility was improving over southern England. The Dorniers and Junkers of KG 76 destined for high level bombing and dive-bombing of Kenley took off, followed shortly by the Heinkels of KG 1.

Roaming some 25 miles ahead of the KG 76 group was an offensive sweep of Bf 109 fighters, some 40 aircraft in all, drawn from III / JG 26 under *Oberleutnant* Gerhard Schöpfel, together with some Bf 109s from JG 3. Close escort for the KG 76 Dorniers was provided by 20 Bf 110s from ZG 26, while the Junkers were under the care of Bf 109s from JG 51. JG 54's Bf 109s, led by *Maj*or Martin Mettig, provided the close escort for the 60 Heinkels of KG 1. The whole armada of bombers with their escorts crossed the Channel in their battle formations at around 12,000 feet. While these units were thus engaged, the specialist 9th *Staffel* of KG 76 was starting to cross the Channel between Dieppe and Beachy Head at wave top height. They hoped to avoid detection at least until their landfall west of Beachy Head, where they would head up the Ouse valley towards Lewes and the London-Lewes railway line which they would use to guide them to their target.

After spending the morning at their forward base at Hawkinge, 501 Squadron was heading back to Gravesend, anticipating another quiet afternoon after the previous day's comparative calm. It was not to be. Before they reached Gravesend, they were ordered over Canterbury at 20,000 feet. They were soon followed by eight more squadrons from a variety of airfields around London – their purpose to intercept the force that was approaching from France. Five of these, including 501 Squadron, were to patrol the Canterbury – Margate line to protect the installations along the Thames Estuary and the airfields to the north of it. The remaining four squadrons were given orders to patrol high over the important sector airfields of Biggin Hill and Kenley.

At the head of III /JG 26 in loose hunting formation, *Oberleutnant* Gerhard Schöpfel, *Staffelkapitän* of the 9th Staffel, glimpsed the Hurricanes of 501 Squadron as they moved towards Canterbury, gradually gaining height in a wide spiral with their sections in standard vic formation. In a bold move typical of many of the experienced hunters in the *Jagdwaffe*, Schöpfel signalled to his pilots to remain at their current height while he manoeuvred into the sun to dive on the unsuspecting Hurricanes. He gambled on the probability that a single aircraft would be less conspicuous than a *schwarm* or a *staffel* in the glare of the sun.

As the Hurricane formation turned away from his position, he rolled "Yellow 1", his Bf 109 E-4, to dive on the two Hurricanes that were acting as weavers slightly above the rest of 501 Squadron. Opening fire, he managed to shoot down both aircraft without attracting the others' attention, so he continued to close on the main group. The rear aircraft soon went down in flames while the rest of the formation continued to climb, unaware of their losses. Intent on getting close to open fire on a fourth Hurricane flown by Pilot Officer Kenneth "Hawkeye" Lee, wreckage from the doomed Hurricane smashed into Schöpfel's propeller and oil covered his windscreen, obscuring his vision and leaving him no alternative but to dive away from the encounter.

Surrounded bt members of his ground crew, Oberleutnant Gerhard Schöpfel sits in His Messerschmitt Bf 109 E-4 "Yellow 1" before final preparations for the next sortie. By the 18th of August, the German Expert had 12 confirmed victories showing on the rudder of his aircraft.

The Hurricanes he shot down were all written off, with one pilot killed, two wounded and one badly wounded. Pilot Officer Lee had been leading the Squadron on this patrol and had assigned the role of weaver to two newcomers so that they could gain valuable experience. It was a decision that he came to regret. Despite being wounded in the right leg, Lee managed to bale out of his machine as it caught fire. He landed awkwardly, not just the result of his wounded leg, but also because when he landed, he was suspected by an elderly armed civilian of being one of the *Luftwaffe* fliers. The situation was resolved by some nearby soldiers who conducted Lee to the bar of the local golf course while he waited for an ambulance. One of the golf club members apparently took exception to this non-member at the bar dripping blood, particularly since the disturbance of the overhead machine gun fire had upset one of his putts.

As Schöpfel pulled away and the wreckage of his victims fell on the Kent countryside below, the rest of JG 26 dived on 501 Squadron and an inconclusive dogfight followed. Thus ended the first major encounter of what became an eventful day for both sides of the conflict. It had demonstrated that even experienced 11 Group squadrons needed to become more aware of the growing threats in the increasingly dangerous skies over Kent and the rest of southern England, something that was to become even more important one week later.

Soon after 1320 hours, the 9th *Staffel's* low-level Dorniers were approaching Kenley from the south, having followed the Lewes-London railway line most of the way. Still hoping that their approach had gone unnoticed, the group was unaware that they had been reported by various Observer Corps. posts along the route they had followed northwards. *Hauptmann* Joachim Roth, the *Staffelkapitän* and navigator for the sortie, became concerned that, with only a minute or so to go before they would be over Kenley airfield, there was no sign of the smoke and debris rising from damage caused by the other groups of dive-bombers and high level bombers from KG 76 that should have already left their mark on Kenley.

He was unaware that the two other KG 76 units had encountered heavy cloud below 10,000 feet over Calais as they started to form up with their fighter escorts. This had disoriented the groups of aircraft as they climbed through the cloud and it took additional time reforming once they were in the open sky. Critically, this delayed the high level bombers by some six minutes from their planned timetable. It doesn't sound much, but curiously, the Dornier formation also overtook the Junkers Ju 88 group that was initially planned to make the first strike against Kenley. Roth's Dorniers were supposed to deliver the *coup de grâce* five minutes after both the dive-bombers and high level bombers had left the area. Instead of this, they were the first to attack the airfield, which had been forewarned of their approach by the Observer Corps. which had tracked them all the way from landfall at Beachy Head, so the airfield's defences were primed and waiting.

Kenley was heavily damaged during the raid, the bulk of it being at the hands of Roth's 9th *Staffel*, which itself suffered heavy casualties from both the airfield's fixed defences and the Hurricanes that had been vectored over the area to intercept them. The high level bombing runs made as the remaining Dorniers of I and III / KG 76 pressed home their attack in the wake of the low level raid added to the destruction.

When the Junkers Ju 88s of II / KG 76 finally approached the area, Kenley was hidden from view by the smoke and debris of the earlier attacks, so they abandoned their dive-bombing attack on the Surrey airfield and turned back over Kent to hit their secondary target, the airfield still under construction at West Malling. They dropped their bomb loads there, causing further damage to the buildings already under repair from earlier raids, demolishing a blister hangar and destroying three Westland Lysanders of 26 Squadron's "A" Flight.

While the various elements of KG 76 were receiving the massed attentions of most of the squadrons that had been patrolling the Biggin Hill and Kenley areas, the 60 Heinkel He 111s of KG1 approached Biggin Hill. Their fighter escort from JG 54 succeeded in keeping Spitfires from 610 Squadron away from the bombers which were stepped up in groups between 12,000 and 15,000 feet. Although KG 1 had anticipated heavy resistance both from RAF fighters and AA fire, even the latter was strangely absent, the local section of the 58th Heavy Anti-Aircraft Regiment having been told to hold their fire since British fighters were operating in the area.

In this way, KG 1 was allowed an almost unhindered run in over Biggin Hill to release its bombs and turn back for home. The damage on this occasion was limited to the landing ground rather than the airfield's buildings, many of the bombs falling in the woods to the east of the airstrip.

The unit's Heinkels didn't escape without casualties however. *Leutnant* Rudolf Ahrens was flying on his first operational mission with the 1st *Staffel* / KG1 in "*Gustav-Karl*" (aircraft code V4+GK). He had the misfortune to encounter engine problems en route to the Channel before crossing to England but felt unable to turn back since this was his first sortie. Inevitably, his aircraft had fallen behind and curiously wasn't picked out for special attention by JG 54 which was concentrating on the main bomber force. As he flew on over Kent, his lone aircraft was spotted by five Spitfires from 65 Squadron which proceeded to use it for target practice, damaging the left engine which Ahrens was obliged to shut down. He turned for home but with all of the RAF fighters quartering Kent airspace on the lookout for any retreating German aircraft, his prospects of regaining the French coast diminished rapidly. Near Ashford, he was attacked by Squadron Leader Mike Crossley of 32 Squadron.

> *I did a quarter attack on it and after about five seconds there appeared*
> *to be an internal explosion, and masses of bits flew off all around.*
> In addition to damaging the right engine which Ahrens rapidly shut down,

Crossley had hit the Heinkel's oxygen bottles which exploded like grenades, wounding the flight engineer and blowing out the plexiglass surrounding the cockpit area. Ahrens then crash-landed the crippled Heinkel at Snargate near Dymchurch, where the crew of five were taken prisoner. *Unteroffizier* Gericke had been badly wounded and later died in Rye Hospital.

Throughout all of this, RAF fighters were crossing swords with the *Jagdwaffe* escorts which fiercely protected the bomber formations under their charge. During the attacks on these two major airfields in the early afternoon of the 18th of August, the RAF squadrons that operated over Kent lost 14 Hurricanes destroyed with three damaged, as well as two Spitfires destroyed and two damaged. Despite the high number of Hurricanes that were written off in these engagements, only three pilots were killed, while a further ten suffered wounds or burns of one degree or another. These losses exclude other aircraft which may have been engaged over Kenley but did not penetrate into Kent.

A group shot of Squadron Leader Mike Crossley's 32 Squadron. Left to right from the back P/O Pfeiffer, F/Lt. Humpherson, F/Lt. Gardner, S/Ldr. Crossle,y F/O Grice, P/O Pain, F/O Eckford, P/O Pniak and P/O Wlasnowolski.

The large number of RAF fighter squadrons that had been scrambled to meet the incoming radar plots accounted for the serious losses that the *Luftwaffe* units suffered during this early afternoon engagement over Kent and Surrey. The radar plots that were recorded as the German forces built up over Calais had been somewhat overestimated, recorded as a mass of some 350 aircraft when in reality it was about 260. This may have been part of the reason why the German's reception committee was so large, even though some of the squadrons patrolling the Canterbury – Margate line didn't engage until the German force was withdrawing.

Whatever the reason, the German losses over Kent were demoralising. Aircraft that came down in parts of Britain other than Kent are not included in this tally, although those that either ditched in the Channel or limped back to France are taken into account since their damage was probably due to action over the county. Using these criteria, it was the Bf 110s of ZG 26 operating as the bombers' close escort that suffered heavily. On the 18th of August, the *Luftwaffe's* heavy fighter was to demonstrate how unwieldy it could be in this role. Of the 20 aircraft that initially joined up with bombers over Calais, seven were shot down over Kent in the early afternoon, with four pilots and six gunners killed, three pilots taken POW, along with one of the gunners. Five of the aircraft lost came from a single *Staffel*, the 6th, virtually wiping it out. It was the first significant loss of these aircraft over Kent, losses that were to be duplicated in other parts of the southeast over the coming weeks.

As the Bf 110s withdrew from Kenley across Kent, covering the Dorniers that had completed the second raid on Kenley, they came under concerted attack from the Spitfire and Hurricane squadrons that had been positioned over Biggin Hill and Kenley. *Oberleutnant* Rüdige Proske, *Gruppen Adjutant* of I / ZG 26 had dived down with the rest of the *Stabschwarm* to head off an attack by elements of Squadron Leader Mike Crossley's Hurricanes from 32 Squadron, some of whom were heading for the retreating Dorniers and some heading for the Bf 110s of his own *Gruppe*. Probably intent on the more obvious threat, he was unaware that Spitfires from Squadron Leader Don MacDonnel's 64 Squadron had dived unseen from their orbit overhead at 20,000 feet and were climbing up from beneath the rear of his group of heavy fighters.

Leutnant Hans-Joachim Kästner was flying as close escort to the Dornier bombers attacking Kenley from high level. He managed a good force landing on St Mary's Marsh, Blackmanstone at about 1335 hours.

MacDonnell selected what he took to be a Dornier bomber (both the Do 17 and the Bf 110 had twin fins and the latter were frequently taken for the former) and commenced firing at Proske's Bf 110 from a distance of 250 yards, closing quickly to

150 yards. He seriously damaged the right engine and started the left engine smoking as well.

This came as a complete surprise both to Proske and his gunner, *Unteroffizier* Hans Mobius, who was badly injured in the legs, and the pilot responded by opening his throttles wide and removing his hands and feet from the controls to put the aircraft in a seemingly uncontrolled spin. It was enough to convince both MacDonnel and Proske's colleagues that his machine was doomed, with the pilot either dead or wounded.

Proske finally managed to regain control after passing below 6,000 feet with both engines smoking and badly damaged, but still operating. However, as he crossed the coast near Dungeness, both engines had given all they could and burst into flames, leaving him no alternative but to put the aircraft down quickly and on land rather than water due to the injuries to his gunner. Narrowly clearing some high tension cables, he managed to make a heavy crash-landing at Dering Farm, Lydd at 1345 hours. He was fortunate to recover quickly from the impact and pulled his injured colleague from the wreck to take cover in a nearby ditch, where they were soon taken prisoner by troops from a nearby AA position.

Oberleutnant Proske's Messerschmitt Bf 110 C-4 under examination near Lydd after the four MG 17 machine guns had been removed from the nose section.

The Bf 109s were not so badly hit, three being lost from JG 3 which had been operating along with JG 26 in advance of the bomber groups. Two more JG 3 aircraft limped back to France to crash or force land there, having suffered combat damage over Kent.

The bombers that targeted Kenley and Biggin Hill inevitably took heavy losses, particularly the Dorniers of the 9th *Staffel* / KG 76, which had been the first to arrive over Kenley. Of the four bombers lost over Kent, three were from the low level raiders. Seven managed to regain the French coast with battle damage and of these, three were from the 9th *Staffel*. The other bomber groups were not immune to loss, two Junkers Ju 88s and one Heinkel He 111 being destroyed, with one of each type suffering damage before returning to their French base. Of these bomber losses, two stand out for different reasons.

The first of these is the lead Dornier Do 17 which made the low level attack on Kenley, flown by *Oberleutnant* Rudolf Lamberty with *Staffelkapitän* Joachim Roth alongside as navigator. After dropping their bomb load on the airfield, Lamberty rapidly pulled the aircraft up to avoid the parachute cable defence rockets that had been deployed to snag unsuspecting enemy aircraft. As he did this, his left wing was hit by a Bofors shell from the airfield defences, holing the fuel tank which immediately caught fire, the self-sealing tank being unable to deal with a 40 mm hole.

Continuing southeast in an effort to get away from the area, Lamberty flew low with the fire burning fiercely in his left wing. Losing the wing would have been fatal, but it was not the only problem. The Hurricanes of 111 Squadron from Croydon were falling on the Dorniers as they all followed the same course, and a succession of the Hurricane pilots took their turn to rake the doomed bomber. As their bullets thudded into the German bomber's structure, the three crewmen in the rear of the cockpit area baled out, two of them realising too late that the aircraft was too low for their parachutes to deploy fully, landing on British soil with multiple injuries. The third, radio operator *Feldwebel* Hugo Eberhart, realised the problem and released his parachute before vacating the escape hatch, the slipstream dragging him from the aircraft and leaving him with minor injuries to his hand.

Anxious to get the blazing Dornier down before the main spar disintegrated in the inferno that was progressively consuming the left wing, Lamberty selected a stubble field and put the aircraft down hard, finally coming to a stop amid clouds of dust. Roth managed to extricate himself from the burning wreck first, followed with some difficulty by Lamberty who suffered severe burns to his hands in making his escape. It was still only 1330 hours.

Over time, Lamberty's Dornier has become immortalised as the "Leaves Green Dornier", coming down as it did at that location, close enough to Biggin Hill for its crew to be at some risk from collateral damage from the high level attack from KG 1's Heinkels.

For completely different reasons, the second bomber casualty that bears some examination is a Junkers Ju 88 of the 5th *Staffel* / KG 76 that was part of the force that should have arrived first at Kenley, performed a dive-bombing attack and withdrawn just before the other KG 76 units arrived. On the approach to their secondary target of West Malling, *Oberfeldwebel* Eichorn's Ju 88 had been hit in one engine by AA fire and, trailing smoke, began to fall behind the unit's formation, making it an irresistible target for the marauding RAF fighters that had arrived in the area, intent on bringing down some of the raiders. Eichorn's crippled Ju 88 was separated from the rest of the KG 76 formation by a Hurricane from 32 Squadron flown by Pilot Officer Boleslaw Wlasnowolski, whereupon it was attacked by a succession of at least five other pilots from different squadrons, most in Hurricanes but some in Spitfires. Unable to withstand such concerted attacks, Eichorn's aircraft finally crashed in flames near the church at Ide Hill, a few miles south of Biggin Hill.

The burnt out remains of Oberleutnant Rudolf Lamberty's Dornier at Leaves Green near Biggin Hill, clearly showing the potential disaster that would have befallen the pilot and crew if they had failed to land when they did. (Via Goss)

Apart from the sad loss of all crew on board, what's intriguing about this casualty is that, unsurprisingly, all six pilots put in a claim for the destruction of a bomber (sometimes misidentified). Most of these claims confirmed the victim had been under attack by various combinations of Hurricanes and Spitfires, and their victim could only have been Eichorn's aircraft since there were no similar casualties close by. However, it seems that no fewer than three of the pilots, including Wlasnowolski, were awarded kills and the three other pilots were each awarded a half-kill. On this basis, it's easy to see how claims could frequently bear little relation to actual losses, since this one Junkers Ju 88 was effectively counted as four and a half aircraft lost. It was an element of confusion that affected both sides of the conflict throughout the battle, particularly British pilots attacking German bombers that normally withstood a lot of punishment before succumbing.

The German fighter casualties from this action also hold some intriguing stories. Oberleutnant Helmut Tiedmann, Staffelkapitän of JG 3's 2nd Staffel had been part of the offensive sweep that had preceded the bombers approaching Kenley and Biggin Hill in conjunction with III / JG 26. His Bf 109 E-4 "Black 13" was hit in the coolant system during one of his encounters with the British fighters that were operating over the area in the early afternoon. He was forced to shut down his engine and force land his aircraft near Leeds Castle, not far from Maidstone. Landing as he did, without a reception committee from the Home Guard already in attendance, he lost no time in moving rapidly away from the crash. Despite the numerous Luftwaffe aircraft which came down in the area at the time and the resultant watchful attention on potential escapees from both the civilian and military, Tiedmann surprisingly managed to evade capture for 12 hours before eventually giving himself up as a POW.

With hay stacked over it to disguise the damaged aircraft from German observers, Oberleutnant Tiedmann's Messerschmitt Bf 109 E-4 lies in the fields near Leeds, Maidstone while the pilot continues to evade capture. (Via Goss)

To supplement the original escort fighters attached to the bomber groups, 16 Bf 109s of the 2nd and 3rd *Staffeln* / JG 52 had been assigned to meet the returning bombers and escort them home. Having completed this by about 1400 hours, their leader, *Oberleutnant* Wolfgang Ewald decided an offensive sweep was in order over Kent. They arrived over Manston at 1420 hours and caught the Spitfires of 266 Squadron on the ground refuelling. The Bf 109s carried out two rapid strafing runs, damaging a Hurricane of 17 Squadron, two Spitfires and severely damaging a further six Spitfires. The RAF ground crews who were servicing the aircraft lost one killed and 15 injured. It was yet another unlucky day for 266 Squadron which had suffered badly two days earlier. Many of the Spitfires destroyed and damaged during this attack had only been delivered brand new the previous evening and had been brought to readiness overnight by the Squadron's fitters. It was the second time in three days that Ewald had managed to bring chaos to the airfield at Manston through surprise strafing attacks at this exposed site.

Coinciding with the latter stages of the Kenley and Biggin Hill raids in the early afternoon, *Luftlotte 3* was mounting its own series of missions in the west, but these were focused on smaller Naval Air Stations operated by Coastal Command, along with other test and training facilities at locations such as Gosport, Ford and Thorney Island. All of these had little to connect them with Fighter Command, even though some of them were used as bases for Coastal Command's attacks on harbours and other installations in northern France. They also chose to attack the radar station at Poling near Littlehampton, all of these attacks being made by Junkers Ju 87 Stuka dive-bombers with appropriate Bf 109 fighter escorts operating at the extremes of their fuel-limited range.

After these attacks, both *Luftflotte 2* and the 11 Group fighter squadrons around southeast England needed time to recover. However, more was to come and this took the form of two main attacks from Kesserling's forces against two important Fighter Command sector stations, Hornchurch and North Weald in Essex. While the targets themselves were well north of Kent, weather conditions conspired to place both forces over the Thames Estuary and Kent with numerous casualties from both sides coming down in and around the county during these sorties.

By 1700 hours, 50 Heinkel He 111s from KG 53 were forming up over the Pas de Calais – their designated target was North Weald, the more northerly of the two airfields that were to be hit in the late afternoon. Their close escort was 20 Bf 110s from ZG 26, already struggling to recover from their punishment during the earlier escort sortie covering the bombers that had attacked Biggin Hill. The combined force of bombers and heavy fighters flew due north across the Channel and instead of crossing Kent itself, proceeded well away from the Kent coast until they were due east of North Weald, at which point they turned west and headed for the target.

As the North Weald force turned west to head for their target, a second group left the Calais area to cross the Kent coast around Deal and head directly up the Thames Estuary towards their target, the sector airfield at Hornchurch. Almost sixty Dornier Do 17s from Johannes Fink's KG 2 were escorted by a mass of Bf 109s from most of the fighter units now using bases around Calais. Close escort was provided by 25 aircraft from JG 51, with almost 100 Bf 109s from JG 3, JG 26, JG 52 and JG 54 operating as high level escort, offensive sweeps ahead of the bomber formation, as well as in the more detached escort role.

The British radar plots and Observer Corps. reports were more accurate than earlier in the day in assessing the size of these two groups and ordered 11 Spitfires and 33 Hurricanes to scramble and patrol the Canterbury – Margate line to make initial contact with the incoming raiders. In all, a total of 13 squadrons from 11 Group and a further four from neighbouring 12 Group were either scrambled or brought to readiness to counter the threat from both attacks. This amassed a force of almost 50 Spitfires and nearly 100 Hurricanes on a broad front from Essex in the north to Kent in the south.

The Heinkels heading for North Weald were intercepted initially by the airfield's own 56 Squadron Hurricanes which divided into sections, some to attack the fighters and some the bombers. They were soon joined by Spitfires from 54 Squadron and the combined force ploughed into the Heinkels and their Bf 110 escorts. The heavy fighters had been operating either side of the bomber groups, initially hampered by the need to maintain formation with the much slower bombers. As soon as the British fighters moved in however, they accelerated to their normal attack speed which was not far off the top speed of both the two types of British fighters. However, the *Zerstörers* were a poor match for both the Hurricane and Spitfire in a turning fight, hampered by their size and wing loading.

The Bf 110s nevertheless gave a good account of themselves and only one of the Heinkels which force landed on Foulness Island had fallen victim to the circling British fighters by the time weather conditions deteriorated sufficiently to make further progress towards North Weald pointless. Between 1700 and 1730 hours, the low cloud that had progressively been moving from the northwest had almost completely covered the area over both North Weald and Hornchurch, with the cloud base falling to as little as 3,500 feet. Denied the chance of accurate bombing from their usual altitude, the Heinkel force manoeuvred onto a reciprocal heading at the same time as almost 30 Hurricanes from 85, 151 and 46 Squadrons were getting into position to make a head-on attack against the German formation.

Both the British pilots and observers on the ground ignored the building cloud and took solace from the sight of the Heinkels apparently turning away in the face of the new threat from this group of Hurricanes. The new arrivals lost no time in setting off after the retreating formation as they passed out into the North Sea and Thames Estuary heading for France and Belgium.

The Heinkels of KG53 were still hampered in their retreat by the 4,400 pounds of bombs each was carrying and would escape from their RAF tormentors quicker without the weight penalty they represented. They unloaded their bombs over Shoeburyness, hitting the barracks and railway station. As the German force withdrew, it wasn't long before the British fighters had expended the 15 seconds' worth of ammunition held by their Brownings' magazines.

While most of the *Luftwaffe* casualties from this encounter fell either in Essex or the North Sea off the Essex coast, several made it to out to sea off the Kent coast. The Hurricanes from 85 Squadron were among the last to engage the retreating German formation and Flight Lieutenant "Hammy" Hamilton managed to avoid the attentions of the Messerschmitt escorts to fire a five second burst of gunfire at the Heinkel flown by *Unteroffizier* Wilhelm Grasser of III / KG 53. His bomber had already been under attack from various other fighters over the preceding 15 minutes. Hamilton's attack seems to have been the final blow since the bomber's undercarriage dropped down and the engines were leaving a heavy black smoke trail as Hamilton broke away to return to base. Grasser could not keep the Heinkel in the air for long and he eventually ditched in the sea somewhere off Ramsgate on a track from Clacton to Ostend. He and his four companions managed to scramble from the sinking aircraft and inflate their dinghy. They were picked up and taken prisoner the following day after spending an uncomfortable night soaking wet but alive.

ZG 26 again suffered a number of casualties in the face of the fierce opposition they encountered at the hands of the various RAF squadrons they came up against in defending the bombers. Four were definitely lost, with as many as five others returning to France with heavy battle damage. Two of the *Zerstörers* that failed to return were shot down into the Channel off the Kent coast.

When North Weald's 56 Squadron first made contact with the raiders before they turned for home, Squadron Leader "Minnie" Manton had followed one of the Bf 110 escorts as it dived to evade the incoming Hurricanes and watched his fire hitting the German aircraft. He lost sight of his descending target as it made off to the south trailing the tell tale sign of white glycol fumes, indicating the aircraft's cooling system had been hit. This was a 4th *Staffel* aircraft flown by *Unteroffizier* Heinz Jäckel and his gunner/radio operator, *Unteroffizier* Theodor Rutters. As they flew low over the Thames Estuary intent on regaining the safety of the French coast, they passed at low altitude over the airfield at Eastchurch on the Isle of Sheppey. The Bofors gunners of the 12th Light Anti-Aircraft Regiment opened fire and hit the passing Bf 110 with a burst of fire, sending it into a shallow dive to crash some two miles east of the airfield at Leysdown on Sea. Jäckel was killed in the crash, but Rutters was thrown clear and taken POW.

A second Bf 110 from the same *Staffel* was brought down by the Hurricanes of 85 Squadron and crashed into the sea off North Foreland. The pilot, *Feldwebel* Friedhelm Gierga was rescued and became a POW, but his gunner, *Unteroffizier* Gerhard Baar, was killed.

At 17.30 hours I was ordered up with my squadron to intercept bogeys. Enemy were spotted at 15,000 east of Thames estuary. The squadron was given tally-ho. I picked out a Me110. After about one and a half minutes of steep turning I delivered a frontal attack on it from a height of 2,000 above it, opening fire at 100-150 yards above it.

It was a burst of about four seconds. I saw smoke coming from both its engines as it glided down from 8,000ft to strike the sea about 40 miles out. After giving various other EA short bursts I delivered another frontal attack on another ME 110, which broke up at about 3,000ft. The rear gunner or pilot baled out. This attack took place at 5,000ft, about 60 miles due east of Margate. Only one person baled out. The aircraft broke up making a series of splashes in the sea. Enemy casualties: two ME 110s destroyed."

While these venomous encounters were unfolding over Essex and the northern sector of the Thames Estuary, the Dornier's of Johannes Fink's KG 2 were moving westwards past Whitstable and over the Isle of Sheppey. Near Canterbury, the Hurricanes of 32 and 501 Squadrons had been gamely trying to get past the massed Bf 109 escorts to get in amongst the bombers. However, they were unable to evade the attentions of the bombers' close escort from JG 51, as well as JG 26 and the other units that had been providing the bombers with cover. This defence was so effective that the Dorniers returned to base with some damage but no recorded losses, despite the best efforts of the RAF pilots and the fifteen AA gun batteries defending the naval dockyard at Chatham.

Flight Lieutenant Pete Brothers (3ʳᵈ from right), relaxing between sorties at Hawkinge with other pilots from 32 Squadron. Pilot Officer Keith Gillman is seen second from the left.

Faced with the deteriorating weather over the northern side of the Thames Estuary, KG 2 turned for home east of Chatham, unknowingly managing to avoid more Hurricanes from 111 Squadron and Spitfires from 64 Squadron that had been waiting for them over the eastern outskirts of London. As they passed back over Deal en route to their French bases, some of the Dorniers left the main formation to bomb the Royal Marine Barracks in the town. While KG 2 returned to base comparatively unscathed on this occasion, the same was not true either for their escorts or the Hurricane pilots of 32 and 501 Squadrons. As 32 Squadron made a bee-line for the Dorniers while they were still en route to Hornchurch, its pilots were frustrated by the Messerschmitts of III / JG

26 which quickly came down from their escort position to block the Hurricanes' attacks on the bombers. Flight Lieutenant Pete Brothers, a well-known face on TV commentary on the Battle of Britain until he died in December 2008, was flying one of the Hurricanes in Squadron Leader Mike Crossley's unit and he later commented:

> *We broke formation as they came in and opened fire and I turned sharply right, on to the tail of an Me 109 as he overtook me..........I gave a quick glance behind me to ensure that there was not another on my tail, laid my sight on him and fired a short burst. It hit him, another short burst and he caught fire and his dive steepened. I followed him down, he went into a field at a steep angle and a cloud of flame and black smoke erupted.*

This was possibly the Bf 109 E-1 flown by *Leutnant* Gerhard Müller-Dühe, the 7th *Staffel* pilot who had shot down the 54 Squadron Spitfire of Ralph Roberts three days earlier outside Calais. The German's aircraft was probably also hit by Pilot Officer Boleslaw Wlasnowolski and it crashed inverted in a wood near Chilham. A second 7th *Staffel* aircraft, "White 13", was brought down at Kingston, near Canterbury. The aircraft and its pilot, *Leutnant* Walter Blume, had been the target of three different 32 Squadron pilots and he was taken POW severely injured.

JG 26 reacted quickly by shooting down three of the British unit's Hurricanes, including that flown by Mike Crossley. All three pilots managed to bale out of their stricken Hurricanes with two suffering from burns.

While 32 Squadron were crossing swords with JG 26, 501 Squadron was embroiled in a struggle with the bombers' close escort unit, JG 51, which conducted a successful defensive operation as far as their charges were concerned. Flight Lieutenant George Stoney made a determined run at the bombers without joining in the melée in which his comrades were embroiled. *Hauptmann* Josef "Joschko" Fözö dispassionately observed the bravery of the lone Hurricane's headlong charge towards the Dorniers of KG 2 before Stoney was shot down and killed.

During this engagement, two of the Squadron's Polish pilots, Flying Officer Stefan Witorzenc and Pilot Officer Pawel Zenker each managed to shoot down a Bf 109 from JG 51. Witorzenc is credited with the loss of *Leutnant* Hans-Otto Lessing, while his countryman, Zenker, managed to deny the *Luftwaffe* the use of another *Jagdwaffe* star, Horst "Jakob" Tietzen. As *Leutnant*, he was the *Staffelkapitän* of the 5th *Staffel* of JG 51 with a tally of 20 kills during the Battle of Britain, as well as seven from the Spanish Civil War. His was a damaging loss for JG 51 and the *Jagdwaffe* generally. Tietzen was posthumously awarded the *Ritterkreuz* and promoted to the rank of *Hauptmann* on 20 August, some time before his body was washed up in France a few weeks later. A further victim of this engagement was *Oberleutnant* Richard Leppla of I / JG 51, who managed to regain the French coast and made a wheels-up landing at St. Inglevert, emerging unhurt from the wreckage of his damaged aircraft.

Darkness fell just before 2100 hours on what must have seemed for many on both sides a long and hard fought day, with much of the day's activities occurring over and around Kent, as well as a decisive series of attacks in the west. Its description as "the Hardest Day" was fully justified since the afternoon engagements were prolonged and bloody. Despite the contemporary propaganda claims of both sides, neither emerged particularly on top.

Leutnant Horst Tietzen, pictured by his Messerschmitt Bf 109 E in its camouflaged blast pen at Marquise a few days before his final mission on the 18th of August 1940. (Via Goss)

It's possible to see the day's results as a minor triumph for the RAF since they demonstrated to the *Luftwaffe* that in order to achieve the air superiority to which Hitler and Göring aspired, it would be at a horrendous cost to the German Air Force in general, but more specifically for its fighter arm, the *Jagdwaffe*. The action over Portsmouth and the other targets in the west also showed that the Stukas could only play a successful role over England with huge fighter protection, a luxury that was rapidly becoming more difficult as the *Jagdwaffe* losses mounted. From this day, the infamous dive-bombers were virtually withdrawn from the action in order to retain their strategic value for the potential invasion. Their effectiveness against shipping targets and as flying artillery for the infantry on the ground could perhaps again repeat the successes they had achieved earlier in the war, once the *Luftwaffe* had gained what was proving an elusive aim, air superiority over southern England.

August
Thinking Again

19th August 1940

Overcast with drizzle around midday had a calming effect on the level of *Luftwaffe* incursions made over Britain at the start of the new week. This also reflected the exhaustion that both sides felt after the previous day's hectic operations. The level of activity over Kent and the rest of Britain was correspondingly diminished.

The focus of the day's missions was limited to groups of *Jagdwaffe* fighters moving up and down the coastal strip in the hope that they might draw some of the RAF fighter units up and so continue to wear down the effective fighting force represented by Fighter Command. Keith Park kept the bulk of his fighters on the ground, waiting for the re-appearance of the more threatening bomber formations. The German fighters amused themselves by strafing the coastal airfields of Manston and Hawkinge, as well as Biggin Hill and Kenley.

Monday the 19th of August is nevertheless a pivotal day, not in terms of the casualties suffered by either side of the conflict, there being few that resulted from action over any part of Britain, and none that are specific to Kent. The casualties that were recorded during the day in other parts of the country stemmed mainly from simple accidents, reconnaissance missions, night bombing or individual raids made by single aircraft taking advantage of the reduced chances of interception offered by the deteriorating weather. What was important about this particular Monday is that both sides took the opportunity to make an assessment of the effectiveness of the tactics adopted during the preceding week.

Two of the *Jagdwaffe's* leading *experten* (aces), Werner Mölders and Adolf Galland had not participated in the operations over England on the previous day. They had both been summoned by *Reichsmarschall* Hermann Göring to *Karinhall*, his hunting lodge outside Berlin, to celebrate the award to each of them of *das goldene Flugzeugführerabzeichen mit Brillianten* (Pilots' badge with gold and diamonds) and enjoy a day of feasting and hunting in the lodge's grounds.

Taking the first steps to reinvigorate the leadership of the fighter groups, Göring followed up his earlier appointment of Werner Mölders to *Geschwader Kommodore* of JG 51 by promoting Adolf Galland to take over a similar role for the whole of JG 26 instead of simply *Gruppenkommandeur* of III / JG 26. Galland's predecessor, *Major* Gotthardt Handrick, the 1936 Olympic modern pentathlon champion, had taken command of JG 26 towards the end of June, but on the 21st of August he was transferred to take over the *Luftwaffe* mission to Roumania. While only three years older than Galland, he was not one of Göring's favoured few. Handrick apparently felt the best position for him as leader was not at the front of JG 26's formations. He preferred to oversee the disposition of his unit's aircraft from a high altitude and behind the bulk of his *Jagdgeschwader*, a tactical choice which sat unfavourably with Göring's new criteria, where aggression was paramount.

Exhibiting what was perhaps later recognised by many of his contemporaries as his desire to become the *Luftwaffe's* highest scoring ace, Galland is understood to have protested at this change of role, concerned that as *Geschwader Kommodore*, his administrative responsibilities would remove him from flying and limit the opportunities to add to his score. His request was angrily refused.

Paradoxically, and at the same time characteristically, Göring took the opportunity to berate the two pilots for the losses that his bomber forces had suffered over the preceding days, blaming the fighter groups for lack of aggression and failing to protect the bombers effectively. It must have left the two young pilots feeling confused and was probably typical of the mood swings Göring suffered from, perhaps due, among other things, to his prolonged drug addiction. This was the first of many signs of what was Göring's growing lack of understanding of the requirements of modern fighter tactics, despite the skills he himself had shown as a First World War fighter ace.

On the 19th of August, Göring called his senior commanders to another conference at *Karinhall* to lay down new ground rules on how his units should complete the destruction of RAF Fighter Command in order to establish the strategic conditions that would allow Hitler to order an invasion of the British Isles. The timetable for the invasion, dictated by weather, tidal conditions and the time required by the Army and Navy to prepare for it, pointed to mid-September as the next opportunity, so the time left for Göring to make good his promises to Hitler was disappearing fast. He issued a memorandum to the senior *Luftwaffe* commanders that were present, which dwelt on various themes but was summarised as follows.

> *To sum up: we have reached the decisive period of the air war against England. The vital task is to turn all means at our disposal to the defeat of the enemy Air Force. Our first aim is the destruction of the enemy's fighters. If they no longer take the air, we shall attack them on the ground, or force them into battle by directing bomber attacks against targets within the range of our fighters. At the same time, and on a growing scale, we must continue our activities against the ground organisation of the enemy bomber units. Surprise attacks on the enemy aircraft industry must be made by day and by night. Once the enemy Air Force has been annihilated, our attacks will be directed as ordered against other vital targets.*

The document for which this was the conclusion covers a wide range of the issues that Göring and his *OKL* staff had selected as important for the continuation of the war against Britain. The problem of gaining air superiority over southern England in preparation for any invasion depended primarily on the ability of the *Luftwaffe's* fighter arm to decimate RAF Fighter Command. Implicit in this was the role of the *Jagdwaffe* in protecting the *Luftwaffe's* bombers while they were attacking the targets selected by *OKL*.

Following the logic of replacing the leaders at the heads of JG 51 and JG 26, Göring required all units throughout the different *Luftflotten* to start a selection process based on skill and performance, rather than rank. The aim of this was to weed out the older commanders that had perhaps become too cautious to destroy RAF Fighter

Command within the fast-disappearing window of opportunity. For a *Kommodore*, the recommended maximum age became 32, 30 for a *Gruppenkommandeur* and 27 for a *Staffelkapitän*. With few exceptions, all of the unit commanders within the fighter units of *Luftflotte 2*, the principal focus of fighter activity against southern Britain, had been changed by the end of August

Werner Mölders and Adolf Galland in discussion with Hermann Göring during the summer of 1940.

For the next phase of the attacks against Britain, Göring highlighted the problems experienced by two types of aircraft during the recent sorties across the Channel against what had proved a well-defended island. Both of these, the Junkers Ju 87 Stuka and the Messerschmitt Bf 110 *Zerstörer*, had performed their respective roles well during the attacks in Europe of late 1939 and the spring of 1940. However, the barrier formed by the Channel and the readiness of Britain's fighter arm for battle made the assault on Britain a different proposition altogether, something that was only just beginning to dawn on the higher echelons of the *Luftwaffe*.

Over the preceding two weeks, the Stuka units had suffered heavily, more perhaps in the west over Southampton, Portsmouth and Portland than over Kent. They were particularly vulnerable unescorted or when the fighter escorts' attentions were already focused elsewhere by British fighter attacks. There had been around 50 Stuka losses over

107

Britain including those lost on the previous day. In order to conserve what had proved a highly effective mobile artillery platform in a fast-moving land war, the Stuka units attached to *Luftflotte 3* in the west were transferred to *Lufflotte 2*, to be held in reserve pending the start of the invasion. Their role became of only marginal significance until occasional sorties were once more mounted against convoys in the late autumn.

The *Zerstörergeschwadern* presented a more complicated problem. Göring had a special regard for this long-range, heavy fighter and, surprisingly, had not anticipated that it would be so completely outclassed in combat with the single-engine fighters that equipped most RAF fighter squadrons. The losses these units had suffered over the early attacks against Britain underlined that their capabilities generally left much to be desired in this hectic theatre of operations, particularly where their operational orders tied them to close bomber escort.

It had not been quite so bad during July and early August when the targets for the *Kampfgeschwadern* had been Channel convoys and coastal facilities, but once the target focus moved to the bigger airfields away from the coast, the diving retreat used by most *Zerstörer* left them exposed to attack over the Home Counties, particularly from RAF fighters waiting for them over the coastal strip. Between the 12th and the 18th of August, some 90 Bf 110 heavy fighters had been lost on operations across the Channel. Putting this into context, on Eagle Day itself (13th of August 1940), the three *Luftflotten* facing Britain (*Luftflotten 2, 3* and *5*) had approximately 250 serviceable Bf 110 aircraft, including the fighter-bombers of *Erprobungsgruppe 210*. This didn't take into account the heavy fighters then operating as night-fighters in the defence of Germany.

In order to conserve the strength of the *Zerstörergeschwadern*, Göring ordered that the heavy fighters were only to be used on sorties where the limited range of the Bf 109 prevented them from operating . Their involvement in bomber escort sorties against targets north of the Thames or in the West Country over the coming weeks showed that, despite continued heavy losses in many units, these heavy fighters could often operate effectively, both limiting bomber losses and causing casualties among the British fighters that attacked them. These logical principles went by the board as the continued heavy losses among the Bf 109 units progressively meant that there weren't sufficient single engine fighters to meet the growing bomber escort demands for the daylight sorties against Britain.

Like many with an interest in the Battle of Britain, I find it surprising that, having removed the Stuka, his principal pin-point bombing tool, from the order of battle, Göring had not already seen that the successes of the specialist low-level bombing unit, *Erprobungsgruppe 210*, showed that there was a tailor-made opportunity for the Bf 110 in that role. It was something that was taken more seriously a few weeks later, but by then, the Bf 110 units had been further decimated by the increasing fighter escort requirements of later bombing missions. Simplistically, the *Luftwaffe* didn't have sufficient Bf 109s for the demands made on the *Jagdwaffe*, so the heavy fighters had to make up the numbers.

In later memoranda to his commanders, Göring would demand that, when operating as bomber escorts, the fighter units would assign a significant portion of their strength to the role of close escort, operating at the same height and speed as the bombers under their care. This was at the behest of his bomber commanders, whose unit losses increased as the assault intensified, with their crews feeling abandoned by their escorts which were frequently operating above and out of their line of sight. However, his memorandum on the 19th of August outlined two guidelines for fighter operations during bomber escort sorties that showed that he was still prepared to allow his fighter commanders some control over the disposition of their forces.

Instead of laying down precise tactics for the bomber escorts to follow, he left it to the individual unit commanders to decide on what proportions of their strength should operate on offensive sweeps ahead of the bombers, close escort and high level escort. In doing this, he recognised that the conditions presented for individual operational sorties would differ sufficiently to make a rigid plan impractical. At this stage he appeared to have made no specific demands for the fighter units to concentrate on the close escort role to the detriment of their preferred high altitude position.

Following the circulation of this memorandum, almost all of the *Jagdgeschwadern* hitherto operating from bases outside the Calais area, were progressively relocated to small airfields and cleared farmland in the area to optimise their aircraft's fuel range over the critical area of southeast Britain. By the 18th of August, there were some 16 individual *Gruppen* of Bf 109s, together with their *Geschwader Stabs*, at bases around Calais and by mid September a further 10 were to join them.

The other point Göring made that caused some concern among the fighter commanders was that the individual bomber units should always be escorted by the same fighter units in order to avoid the sort of problems that were caused by limited communications between fighter and bomber units early on Eagle Day itself. By operating continuously together, he apparently felt that the problems of not having compatible radio equipment to allow communication between bombers and fighters during operational sorties would be overcome by intuitive understanding, strengthened by social mixing between the different groups.

Unification of radio equipment throughout the *Luftwaffe*, or at least within each of the *Luftflotten* would have seemed a more preferable option. Perhaps this was another area that suffered as a result of overall German material shortages, a general problem throughout the war. It might also have been another example of the problem caused by personal ambitions affecting overall efficiency within the still young military arm of the *Luftwaffe*.

It should also be remembered that during the Spanish Civil War and the years that followed, many of the *Kondor* Legion veterans, including Adolf Galland, had initially been against the installation of any radio equipment in fighter aircraft. This was borne out of the traditional mistrust of new technology, strengthened by the negative impact on performance created by the additional weight of the equipment, always a concern for the fighter pilots whose trump cards were invariably height and speed, elements always threatened by weight.

Göring was not alone in dwelling on the lessons to be learned from the pattern of action over the preceding week. Keith Park, AOC of Fighter Command's No 11 Group covering London and the southeast of England, issued his own guidelines to his sector controllers by means of Instruction No. 14.

The first two weeks of August had demonstrated that the *Luftwaffe* had changed its focus of attack away from the Channel towards targets on the mainland, in particular the airfields that protected the capital. There is no doubt that Park had mixed feelings about this. On the one hand, he must have been relieved since it reduced the exposure of his valuable pilots and aircraft to the dangers of operating over the unforgiving waters of the English Channel. He must also have been grateful since it put more pressure on the German pilots, as they were forced to operate further from their bases and over enemy territory. Conversely, anxiety must have been the other emotion, since the attacks had by now started against his sector airfields, where damage to the vital control rooms would have made much more difficult the task of dispatching the most appropriate reaction from his fighter squadrons against the incoming raids.

A) *Despatch fighters to engage large enemy formations over land or within gliding distance of the coast. During the next two or three weeks, we cannot afford to lose pilots through forced landings on the sea. (Protection of all convoys and shipping in the Thames Estuary are excluded from this paragraph).*

B) *Avoid sending fighters out over the sea to chase reconnaissance aircraft or small formations of enemy fighters.*

C) *Despatch a pair of fighters to intercept single reconnaissance aircraft that come inland. If clouds are favourable, put a patrol of one or two fighters over an aerodrome which enemy aircraft are approaching in clouds.*

D) *Against mass attacks coming inland, despatch a minimum number of squadrons to engage enemy fighters. Our main object is to engage enemy bombers, particularly those approaching under the lowest cloud layer.*

E) *If all our squadrons around London are off the ground engaging enemy mass attacks, ask No. 12 Group or Command Controller to provide squadrons to patrol aerodromes Debden, North Weald, Hornchurch.*

F) *If heavy attacks have crossed the coast and are proceeding towards aerodromes, put a squadron, or even the sector training flight, to patrol under clouds over each sector aerodrome.*

G) *No. 303 (Polish) Squadron can provide two sections for patrol of inland aerodromes, especially while the older squadrons are on the ground refuelling, when enemy formations are flying over land.*

H) *No. 1 (Canadian) Squadron can be used in the same manner by day as other fighter squadrons.*

This circular simply underlined to his group's sector controllers that it was the bombers that were the targets for Fighter Command, although he recognised that the *Jagdwaffe* would have to be dealt with in the process.

It made clear that operations over the Channel were to be avoided in order to protect pilot numbers, and that the controllers should call for assistance from neighbouring 12 Group when required. The latter became a thorny issue over the following weeks, but Park's directive also sets in motion the beginning of the process of absorbing into the operational structure of Fighter Command the first of the "foreign" contingent squadrons.

Air Vice Marshall Keith Park, the New Zealander, who was the principal strategist for 11 Group's defence of southeast England throughout the summer of 1940, a role in which he was successful more times than not.

Hitherto, numerous trained pilots who had fled the German occupation of many European countries, particularly France, Belgium, Holland, Czechoslovakia and Poland, had been absorbed into the complement of established Fighter Command squadrons, in the same way as other volunteers from the Commonwealth countries and even, surreptitiously, the U.S.

Others from mainly non English-speaking countries had been formed into units in which the pilots were all of one nationality, usually under a British Squadron Leader and Flight Commanders. These squadrons had yet to be released for operational duties, some still being trained to fly the modern British fighters, but also since there was a degree of mistrust due to the temperament of some nationalities and the general language problems inherent in controlling their deployment. In releasing 303 (Polish) Squadron for limited operations when required, Park took the first step towards their general use as an operational unit. This particular squadron was put on fully-operational status at the end of August and between then and the end of October became the highest scoring unit throughout Fighter Command. Most of the squadron's pilots were eager to take revenge for the German invasion of Poland and took every opportunity to do this by hunting and killing German crews with zeal.

For all these reasons, while the 19th of August was comparatively uneventful from an active operational perspective, in reality it was a pivotal day in the Battle of Britain. It was on this day that steps were taken that effectively laid the groundwork for the changing pattern of engagements that would take place during the remainder of August and the first days of September.

The *Luftwaffe* entered this next phase with a renewed vigour, stemming significantly from the promotions given to the rising young leaders, who pursued their missions with renewed aggression. At the same time, "Smiling Albert" Kesserling, the commander of the pivotal *Luftflotte 2*, started to employ a wide variety of tactics for attacks on No 11 Group's airfields, frequently giving the Group's controllers problems in deciding how to react to a complex series of separate, but often co-ordinated attacks.

These changes demanded continuous and tiring sorties from both British and German fighter pilots, who now became locked in a vicious war of attrition which caused heavy casualties on both sides. When the weather conditions finally improved on the 24th of August, it soon became clear that Fighter Command's losses were progressively pushing the squadrons in No 11 Group to the point where exhaustion and casualties might have given Göring the prize he wanted – complete air superiority over southeast England.

20th August 1940

Although mainly clear in the southeast and Channel areas, the weather over most of England again began to deteriorate, with rain spreading from the north. Although there were numerous small raids and reconnaissance sorties throughout the day by the *Luftwaffe*, activity was on a reduced scale as the operational groups on both sides absorbed the tactical changes required to address the problems experienced over the previous week or more. This level of relative inactivity would continue during the next three days until the 24th of August when the cloud and squally weather changed to more settled conditions.

Hugh Dowding and Keith Park remained concerned over pilot losses, something that would become progressively more worrying over the next two weeks, but there was less reason to be anxious over replacement aircraft. While there were periods during this time when losses surpassed replacement supply, despite the efforts of Lord Beaverbrook as Minister for Aircraft Production, this was less of a problem for the RAF Fighter Command than it was becoming for the *Luftwaffe*.

On the 20th of August, *Generalfeldmarschall* Erhard Milch, began a five-day tour of the Air Fleets to check on their morale, equipment deficiencies and how Göring's replacement of unit commanders was being implemented. While Milch still held the title of Secretary of State for the Air Ministry, Göring had effectively sidelined this energetic and professional individual away from critical roles in the *Luftwaffe* in favour of men who were more amenable to Göring's fragmented and less organised approach. Typical of these was Ernst Udet, another star from World War One, a renowned pilot and partygoer, but with no administrative or technical skills other than those of a brilliant pilot. In 1939, Udet effectively replaced Milch and was appointed *Luftwaffe* Director-General of Equipment and given the rank of *Generaloberst*. In reality, he wasn't up to the demands of the job and his lack of proficiency probably lay behind many of the problems that the *Luftwaffe* eventually suffered from as missions over England chewed up both fighters and bombers, and crews were lost or wounded.

In a report that he wrote at the end of his inspection tour, Milch made telling comments on serious material deficiencies in terms of front-line aircraft strength, crew and equipment shortages. Even at this comparatively early stage of the assault on the British mainland, he drew particular attention to the growing shortage of pilots, as well as other trained crew. Numerous unit commanders had made comments to him on the poor quality of the new pilots that were arriving in the Pas de Calais fresh from training units. Many of these newcomers had received minimal training in the critical and demanding task of handling the Bf 109, notoriously difficult at low speed and altitude, as well as having very limited training in live firing. There were also clear indications that the young trainees had little experience of the MG FF 20 mm cannon carried in all the "E" variants of this machine apart from the lighter-armed Bf 109 E-1. For many skilled *Jagdwaffe* pilots, it was often these cannons that allowed the Bf 109, as well as the Bf 110, to deliver a knock-out blow more often than was possible with the 7.92 mm MG 17 that was the alternative armament.

Most British fighter pilots would have loved to have had cannons as part of the armament of their Spitfires and Hurricanes. Devastating though they were at very close range, the eight .303 inch Browning machine guns that equipped both aircraft, had no more than 15 seconds of continuous firing before the ammunition ran out, allowing many bombers to return to France. They may have been riddled with holes, possibly with one engine out of action and dead and wounded on board, but many were repaired to fly again and, more importantly the uninjured crew were back operations.

The destructive power of 20 mm calibre cannon was another matter entirely. Although experiments were made with cannons in Spitfires issued to 19 Squadron and a very limited number of individual Hurricanes, there were shortcomings with the cannons' installations and operation that prevented them from playing any constructive role for Fighter Command during the Battle of Britain.

Despite this, it's possible to find contrary views from inside the *Jagdwaffe*. *Oberleutnant* Hans Schmoller-Haldy, one of the *Jagdwaffe* pilots that flew Bf 109s armed with cannons, was able to fly a captured Spitfire during the summer of 1940. He made the following interesting comments that reveal that the German flyers sometimes had their own problems with the cannons and machine guns in their Bf 109s. Schmoller-Haldy was one of the German pilots who flew Bf 109s in the Spanish Civil War, operating with the 3rd *Staffel* /JG 54 during the Battle of Britain and the Russian campaign. He was seriously wounded on the Eastern Front in 1942, but survived the war on Adolf Galland's staff.

For fighter versus fighter combat, I thought the Spitfire was better armed than the Me 109. The cannon fitted to the 109 were not much use against enemy fighters, and the machine guns on top of the engine often suffered stoppages. The cannon were good if you scored a hit, but their rate of fire was very low. The cannon had greater range than the machine guns. But we were always told that in a dogfight one could not hope to hit anything at ranges greater than 50 metres, it was necessary to close in to short range.

What was rapidly turning into a brutal war of attrition between Fighter Command and the *Jagdwaffe* was already having a telling effect on the strength of the German units, perhaps even more at this point than with Fighter Command. The daily toll of killed, missing or wounded personnel on both sides increased rapidly over the days that followed, as did the exhaustion and fears of the pilots taking part in the critical battles to follow. For the German pilots, the mental strain was heightened by the need to cross the Channel on both outbound and inbound legs of each mission, as well as the knowledge that crew brought down over Britain were inevitably sent to the POW camps.

Despite the low level of combat during the morning of the 20th of August, the afternoon witnessed a renewed spate of comparatively small but continuous sorties from the Pas de Calais over Kent. Taking the form of offensive sweeps, strafing and bombing runs on some of the airfields, Eastchurch, West Malling and Manston all found themselves on the receiving end of some of these. By this time, Manston had been all but abandoned due to the severity and regularity of both strafing and bombing attacks, made all the easier for the *Luftwaffe* because of its exposed position. Manston's function would soon become degraded to an emergency landing and refuelling airfield, with minimal AA defences, limited accommodation remaining, numerous bomb craters and many unexploded bombs. Eastchurch continued to receive attention, despite its lack of connection with Fighter Command activities, while West Malling was still largely under construction and a long way from becoming operational as a fighter base. The Dover balloon barrage also came in for another round of attacks.

During the day's operations over Kent and the Thames Estuary, the casualties suffered on both sides were almost at parity. Another Bristol Blenheim night fighter from 600 Squadron, one of the few remaining inhabitants at Manston, was damaged in an attack during mid afternoon. *Feldwebel* Oskar-Heinz Bär of the 1st *Staffel* / JG 51 shot down a Spitfire from Hornchurch's 65 Squadron over the Thames Estuary as it was trying to attack the Dorniers of KG 2 that were aiming for Eastchurch. The Spitfire force landed in Essex on Havengore Island, Foulness, and was written off, but the pilot, Pilot Officer Hart, was unhurt. "Heinrich" or "Pritzel" Bär went on to become one of the leading *Luftwaffe* NCO *experten* in the Battle of Britain with some 17 victories, finishing the war as *Oberst* flying Messerschmitt Me 262 jet fighters with a total tally for the war of 220 victories, mostly on the Eastern front.

KG 2 lost one of the Dornier's from the 9th *Staffel*, brought down during the attack on Eastchurch and crashing at Capel Hill Farm, Leysdown at 1615 hours. The Dornier had probably been brought down by Hurricanes from Kenley's 615 Squadron flown by Squadron Leader Joe Kayll and one of his squadron colleagues. The crew suffered one fatality, *Feldwebel* Rudiger, with the remaining three crew members joining the growing ranks of *Luftwaffe* personnel heading for the POW camps.

From the operations over the Thames Estuary during that afternoon, *Feldwebel* Helmut Maul of I / JG 51 appears to have been the only casualty among the *Jagdwaffe* pilots. Around 1520 hours, he had left his French base at Guines for a sortie over the Thames Estuary, probably as escort for KG 2's Dorniers or an offensive sweep ahead of their attack on Eastchurch. Over the north Kent coast, the engine of his Bf 109, "White 6", was damaged, but he managed to limp back to the Channel coast before ditching in a strengthening swell not far from the English Coast.

It must have been a terrifying experience for Maul. Scrambling out of his rapidly-sinking aircraft, he found that his *Schwimmveste* (life jacket) wouldn't inflate and he was struggling to remain afloat, with the drag of his heavy boots and flying suit making it all the more difficult. Fortunately for him, one of the Heinkel He 59 *Seenotflugkommando* (air-sea rescue) aircraft spotted him in the water, but the crew were cautious about landing to pick him up due to the deteriorating sea conditions. After dropping two life rafts nearby, both of which Maul was unable to reach due to his growing exhaustion, the bi-plane finally landed. A third raft attached to the Heinkel by rope was thrown to him, and he managed to reach it.

His feeling of relief on being hauled into the plane by the crew was comparatively fleeting. The weather had worsened, with the prospect of a storm developing, and the sea state making it impossible for the aircraft to get back into the air. Worse still, one of the Heinkel's engines was soon damaged by an unusually heavy wave and the only chance lay with the radio operator making contact with a friendly boat to rescue them all. He had been continually sending position and status reports once the problem became clear, but the heavy sea was inexorably pushing them towards a minefield.

Fortunately, after three hours drifting and as the light faded, they heard engines and fired a signal flare which drew the rescue boat towards their battered aircraft. They all regained the French coast at dawn the next morning and the Heinkel was recovered badly damaged.

The young German pilot was a lucky man. Two days earlier, during the vicious fighting over the southeast, *Hauptmann* Horst Tietzen, the *Staffelkapitän* of JG 51's 5th *Staffel*, had been shot down in the sea off Whitstable by a Hurricane pilot from 501 Squadron. Recorded as missing, the 20-kill *expert* apparently survived his aircraft's crash, but in desperation at not being found by any of the rescue services from either side, took the only option open to him to curtail the loneliness and suffering he faced. His body was washed up on the French coast some days later with a single bullet wound to the head and his service pistol missing.

Helmut Maul would have been unaware of this sad turn of events at the time of his own force landing in the Channel but it appears that shortly after this, side-arms were banned from operational flights by *Jagdwaffe* pilots.

21st- 23rd August 1940

The stormy weather continued over the next three days and the main thrust of *Luftwaffe* activity centred on *Störangriffen* (nuisance raids), mostly made by single bombers taking advantage of cloud cover to penetrate into many parts of Britain. East Anglia and the western parts of Britain suffered some damage during these incursions, although off the Kent coast, renewed convoy activity under cover of the bad weather led to a flurry of sorties around the vessels involved.

The morning of 22nd of August saw a small convoy (code-named *Totem*) battling its way through the heavy seas in the Dover Straits towards the Thames Estuary. Passing through the Dover Straits between 0800 and 0900 hours, the convoy called for air cover as their naval escort believed they were under *Luftwaffe* attack. At this point during their passage eastwards, it turned out that the waterspouts that the ships saw around them came not from German bombers, but from the heavy guns positioned around Cap Gris-Nez in France. Some 100 shells were said to have been fired with no damage caused and the bombardment was eventually interrupted reportedly through technical problems with the guns.

A coaster steams past the white cliffs around Dover, narrowly escaping from a near-miss from the artillery batteries firing from the French coast.

By early afternoon, the convoy was off Deal, where the two Bf 110 *Staffeln* of the industrious *Erprobungsgruppe 210* endeavoured to launch an attack in the low cloud cover. They were escorted by Bf 109s which caused a number of casualties among the Spitfire squadrons that had by then taken up position on convoy patrol. Despite this, the convoy continued towards the Thames Estuary unscathed by the *Jabos'* attack, while the

German fighter-bombers returned to France frustrated by the defence put up by the convoy's defensive patrols.

Sergeant George Collett of 54 Squadron's "B" Flight was shot down into the sea off Deal at 1315 hours. Sergeant Douglas Corfe of Hornchurch's 610 Squadron suffered a similar fate some time later, crashing in flames at Hawkinge but emerging largely unhurt. Pilot Officer Douglas Hone of Kenley's 615 Squadron had an unfortunate experience in poor visibility with the cloud ceiling at only 1,500 feet. His Hurricane was mistakenly attacked by another Hurricane and he was obliged to make a force landing near Deal at 1315 hours.

The poor visibility must have caused many problems for both sides and it was almost the undoing of one of *Erprobungsgruppe 210's* 2nd *Staffel* Bf 110s. *Unteroffizier* Ernst Glaeske had been returning from the convoy attack when he took up position alongside a "109" that was also heading in the same direction. Much to his horror, this turned out to be a Spitfire which proceeded to rake the right engine of his fighter-bomber before he was able to escape into cloud cover and limp back to Calais-Marck.

Later in the day, it was Manston's turn to suffer the attentions of *Erprobungsgruppe 210* again. *Hauptmann* Hans von Bolstenstern, had become this specialist unit's second *Gruppenkommandeur* following the death of their first commander, Walter Rubensdörffer, on the 15th of August. Von Bolstenstern led his men on another sortie against the battered Kent airfield around 1900 hours. Despite the 30 bombs dropped during this sortie and the damage done to the hangars, stores and offices that remained, Manston's Record Book states that there were no casualties on the ground. The Blenheim night fighters of 600 Squadron finally transferred their operational base from Manston to Hornchurch.

The fighter-bombers had been escorted on this mission by the Bf 109s of JG 26 with Adolf Galland leading his first mission as *Geschwader Kommodore*. Employing tactics that became the trademark of the unit when on escort duty, JG 26 conducted an offensive sweep ahead of the raid, as well as escorting the *Jabos* to and from their target. JG 26 made an effective job of clearing the way through Fighter Command's defences for the fighter-bombers to complete their task. Both 616 Squadron from Kenley and 65 Squadron from Hornchurch each lost a Spitfire to Galland's Bf 109s. On his first engagement with the enemy, Flying Officer Hugh "Cocky" Dundas of 65 Squadron was bounced by a Bf 109 which shot away his controls, as well as damaging his engine and coolant system, setting the aircraft alight. It's possible he'd become the 11th victory claim of *Oberleutnant* Gerhard Schöpfel, *Staffelkäpitan* of the 9th *Staffel* / JG 26. Dundas recounted spinning down from 12,000 feet to 800 feet struggling to open the jammed cockpit hood in order to bale out. Unsurprisingly, he was relieved finally to vacate his burning Spitfire and was later admitted to the Kent and Canterbury hospital with a broken collar bone and leg wounds. His aircraft crashed at Runninghill, near Elham.

One of Cocky's squadron colleagues, Sergeant Michael Keymer, made a tactical error by allowing himself to be chased south over the Channel by *Leutnant* Hans Krug, the *Staffekapitän* of the 4th *Staffel* / JG 26. Sadly he was shot down and killed over

Marquise, on the outskirts of Calais. JG 26 also badly damaged three other Spitfires, with one returning to Hornchurch and two making force landings at battered Manston airfield. None of the pilots were injured.

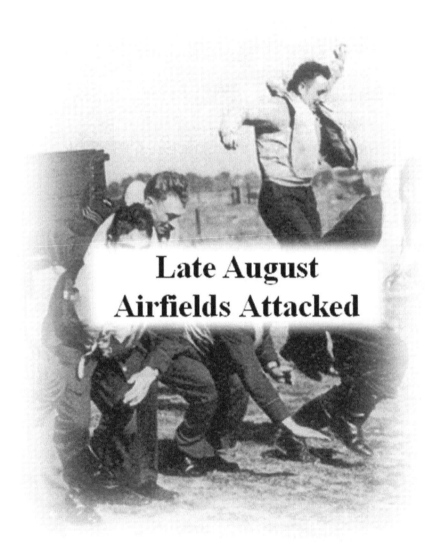

24th August 1940

While the midlands and the north of England were still covered with cloud and showers, the weather over the south and in the Dover Straits had finally improved, with clear skies, hazy sunshine and rising temperatures. It was to be the first day of a new chapter in the German air assault on Britain by the rejuvenated *Luftwaffe* units under their recently-promoted younger leaders, all eager to prove that the faith shown in them was justified. In the days that followed and as the intensity of the fighting increased, both sides would feel the growing burden of exhaustion that this new level of conflict imposed.

By the 24th August, most of the *Jagdwaffe* units that had been based in the west of France as part of *Luftflotte 3* had been transferred to the Pas de Calais. This gave Kesserling's *Luftflotte 2* the maximum possible fighter strength to continue Göring's task of destroying Fighter Command over the southern part of Britain prior to the invasion, still scheduled for the middle of September. Focusing on the ring of major airfields that surrounded London, Kesserling intelligently used every tactic he could think of to draw the British fighters into the air so that his own fighter pilots could shoot them down.

Luftflotte 2's Commander, Albert Kesserling (2nd from left), discusses tactics with some of his command staff on the cliffs overlooking the Dover Straits.

He sent over strong bomber formations escorted by ever larger groups of both Bf 109s and Bf 110s, increasingly using the *Zerstörers* where the targets were beyond the range of the single-engine fighters. In practice, this meant that missions against airfields north of the Thames such as Hornchurch and North Weald depended on the heavy fighters that could go all the way to and from these targets. The Bf 109s' role on these missions was limited to quick offensive sweeps ahead of the bomber groups, penetrating as far as fuel reserves would allow. Their purpose was to tempt British fighters off the ground, at best to be engaged and shot down, and at worst to allow the bombers to catch them on the ground refuelling and rearming. *Jagdwaffe* units also rendezvoused with the bomber groups on their way home as they came back within the operating radius of the Bf 109s. This would often amount to multiple sorties for the Bf 109s. As the offensive gathered pace, it was not uncommon for some units to be flying as many as five or six sorties each day, always over the unforgiving Channel, so increasing the strain and exhaustion felt by most of the pilots.

The aim of all these attacks continued to be degrading Fighter Command's capabilities, primarily by destroying Hurricanes and Spitfires, ideally with their pilots, but also damaging the RAF support structure in terms of airfield facilities, aircraft factories and repair depots. The most tangible of these targets were the airfields themselves and the British fighters that such attacks drew into the air to fight off the incoming raids. Kesserling had already recognised the limited reaction normally drawn from the British fighters when he sent fighter sweeps over the south coast and the Home Counties. Such operations had generally been allowed free rein over the south when the Sector Controllers followed Keith Park's instructions to concentrate on formations with a bomber component. In order to induce the British fighters off the ground, Kesserling therefore sent in limited numbers of bombers with huge fighter escorts.

In yet another subterfuge, other formations, comprising both the twin-engine Bf 110 and the single-engine Bf 109, would be sent north across the Channel. *Zerstörers* had frequently been mistaken both by pilots and the Observer Corps. for the Dornier Do 17 medium bomber. Both aircraft had distinctive twin fins so they were often confusing to identify, particularly from a distance. These fighter sorties would mimic both the height and speed of the medium bombers which usually crossed the Channel at around 180 mph and 15,000 – 18,000 feet, while the fighters would normally be aiming to be above 21,000 feet, cruising at closer to 300 mph while weaving around the slower formation. Fighter formations were normally identified early on by the RDF stations due to their high speed and tendency to go for maximum altitude. Sometimes the trick worked and huge dogfights were the unavoidable result, with both sides suffering losses.

At frequent intervals during the 24th of August, groups of *Luftwaffe* aircraft crossed the Kent coast aiming for targets around the Thames Estuary and the Channel coast. From early morning until late afternoon, there were six separate groups of German raiders that crossed the Channel. The previous day, *Reichsmarschall* Hermann Göring had issued yet another directive to the *Luftwaffe* units facing Britain to exhort them to intensify the assault.

The enemy is to be forced to use his fighters by means of ceaseless attacks.

Under normal circumstances, with Göring several hundred miles away from Calais, either in Berlin or at *Karinhall*, his nearby hunting lodge, it was left to the individual *Luftflotten* commanders, particularly Kesserling in terms of raids on southeast Britain, to translate the rhetoric into results.

Manston, near Ramsgate, continued to receive regular strafing attacks and heavier raids. From the 24th of August, the last of the squadrons using the airfield as a forward base withdrew to less exposed alternatives and all personnel not involved in servicing aircraft or airfield defence were moved elsewhere, finally confirming that the airfield's status had been degraded to an emergency landing ground. During the whole of the Battle of Britain, this most easterly of Kent's airfields remained the only fighter base that the *Luftwaffe* succeeded in shutting down for more than a day or two. For Beppo Schmid's *Luftwaffe* Intelligence Group, Manston wasn't the only fighter base that they concluded had been rendered inoperative as a result of the *Luftwaffe* attacks up to the end of August. They believed Kenley was destroyed on the 18th of August and that Biggin Hill was similarly put out of operation towards the end of August and early September. They were to be proved almost correct as far as Biggin Hill was concerned, with the Kent airfield undergoing almost continuous raids over this period.

Keith Park had already been struggling to find aircraft and, more critically, operationally-fit pilots to maintain a continuous rotation of squadrons available for action, as opposed to those that were resting, refuelling or rearming. One result of this was the transfer on the 22nd of August of another Defiant Squadron to Hornchurch. This was 264 Squadron which had been in 12 Group, based at Kirton-in-Lindsey on the Lincolnshire fens. After the decimation of 141 Squadron's Defiants on the 19th of July, this was a move that smacked of desperation, placing another group of pilots and gunners in jeopardy in their less-than-manoeuvrable heavy fighters. Nonetheless, at 0500 hours on the 24th of August, Squadron Leader Philip Hunter's men were ordered from their new base at Hornchurch to provide fighter cover for Manston airfield, which they would use as a forward base for the rest of the day.

The RDF stations picked up the first raid heading for the coast between Dover and Dungeness around 0830 hours, this later proving to be more than 40 Junkers Ju 88 and Dornier Do17 bombers, with Bf 109 escorts from III / JG 26 and II / JG 51. The target was believed to have been Dover itself, although there are no records of any bombs being dropped. The intruders were intercepted by Spitfires from Biggin Hill's 610 Squadron together with Hurricanes from 85 Squadron based at Croydon.

The Biggin Hill unit recorded the loss of only one of its Spitfires, piloted by a New Zealand Sergeant, Johnny Arnfield. He was attacked by *Hauptmann* Josef Fözö of II / JG 51 off Ramsgate and was forced to bale out when his aircraft caught fire. The Spitfire crashed at Hammill, near Eastry at 0850 hours and the pilot was admitted to the Victoria Hospital in Deal with a broken ankle, later being awarded the DFC.

There were also casualties among the escorts from III / JG 26. One Bf 109 E-4 was shot down into the sea off Margate, wounding the pilot who was rescued by the

Seenotflugkommando. Two others were damaged during this engagement, but managed to return to the French coast, one crash-landing at Caffiers. The other aircraft had been piloted by *Feldwebel* Artur Beese who force landed his Bf 109 E-1 "Yellow 11" on the sand dunes near Calais, breaking its back. Both the aircraft that were brought down on the French coast were sufficiently damaged to be written off.

One of the many Messerschmitt Bf 109s that was obliged to make a force landing on the beaches around the Pas de Calais after sorties over the Channel that left them damaged or out of fuel.

Two more groups of raiders crossed the Kent coast at roughly two-hourly intervals, each heading towards the Dover-Ramsgate area. Shortly after midday, Manston was hit in a series of attacks that the passage of time and possible misidentification of aircraft in the heat of action have confused, so that the sequence and identities of the attackers is still a matter of some debate.

What remains clear is that one attack was made at 1250 hours, at the time when a flight of 264 Squadron's Defiants was patrolling overhead and the remaining aircraft were on the ground refuelling and rearming. The attackers were identified as a group of about 20 Bf 110s with a strong fighter escort. This can only have been *Erprobungsgruppe 210* which succeeded in heavily damaging the remaining buildings on the airfield, as well as severing the all-important telephone lines and damaging several aircraft on the ground. Eminent specialist historians such as John Vasco, who has made a close study of the role of *Erprobungsgruppe 210* in the Battle of Britain, have been able to confirm that the unit did strike Manston in the early afternoon of the 24th of August and got away scot-free.

Perhaps the reason for the confusion over the identities of the raiders that caused such fundamental damage to Manston and the surrounding area is that another formation from II / KG 76 was bombing from their normal height around the same time as the *Jabo* strike. While *Erprobungsgruppe 210* were not immune to causing collateral damage around the targets that they attacked (as in the case of their raid on Croydon on the 15th of August), the damage caused around the airfield and in the village of Manston is perhaps a more credible side effect of bombs dropped from greater height, as would probably have been the case with KG 76's Ju 88s.

The other element that supports the concept of two different groups of attackers hitting the airfield at roughly the same time is the timing of the casualties suffered among the pilots of 264 Squadron who took off to chase the bombers back to France. Four of these are recorded as occurring at 1240 hours, with two of these incidents involving Ju 88s. If the timing of the *Jabo* strike at 1250 is accurate, then it's probable that *Erprobungsgruppe 210* hit the airfield after the KG 76 bombers had turned for home, with the standing patrol from 264 Squadron that was already airborne in hot pursuit. Spitfires from 610 Squadron were also in the Dover area although it's unclear whether they intercepted the bombers. Pilot Officer Eric Barwell, who was the pilot of one Defiant that managed to return to Hornchurch after this action, described the encounter.

> The squadron was sent on patrol and after an inconclusive engagement, landed at Manston to refuel and rearm. We had just completed that but were not ordered up again until we were scrambled in a hurry just as a number of Ju 88s were attacking Ramsgate and the edge of the airfield. We took off in twos and threes but had not time to form up as a Squadron. I had one new crew in my section (PO Jones and PO Ponting) and we chased after the bombers as they headed for France. It was a long stern chase and before we were near enough to engage them, I spotted five enemy fighters. I at once called up Jones, "Bandits! Line astern – evasive action!" and turned as hard as possible as they attacked. Unfortunately, Jones did not turn hard enough and was hit and went down immediately.

> All five aircraft then concentrated on me and as each came in, I turned hard giving my gunner, Sergeant Martin, a straight no deflection shot. I saw strikes on one or two of them and one went down into the sea. On one occasion Martin did not fire – I do not think I swore at him but asked him why. "You blacked me out" was his answer. We were some miles out to sea and it meant I had to keep turning hard as each plane attacked and I began to think that we should never get back to the Kent coast but the attacks ceased.

> I like to think we had damaged the other four aircraft but probably they had run out of fuel or ammunition. We landed back at Hornchurch, but the Squadron had suffered disastrously.

Squadron Leader Hunter and his gunner failed to return after last being seen pursuing the Ju 88s towards France. His loss was to be keenly felt among the surviving aircrew of the Squadron, such was his reputation among his men. One other Defiant was brought down by return fire from the KG 76 gunners and two further Defiants became victims of the bombers' escorts from JG 3, one of which was probably the aircraft described by Eric Barwell. These two casualties may have been victims of *Hauptmann* Günther Lützow who had become the new replacement *Geschwader Kommodore* of JG 3 as of the 21st of August.

As he manoeuvred his *Stabschwarm* around the bomber formation and dived to intercept any British fighters he thought represented a threat to the bombers, he caught sight of a group that had previously escaped his attention.

Just below the foremost Kette there were some fighters. Something seemed to be wrong. One of the bombers veered away from the formation, leaving a long white smoke trail. Dammit. I flew towards the bombers at full speed, then I saw they were English two seater fighters – Defiants.

Unseen, they had approached the bomber formation from below and were now firing into the defenceless bombers with their four machine guns. It would cost them dearly. I got to within 30 metres of the first one and my guns spoke – a volley, and a flame flickered around the enemy's fuselage. Slowly he fell off on one wing – that one wouldn't be coming back. Then I went for the next one. A tight left turn with the throttle wide open and I was already close behind him. I pushed the button and he too started to burn and fall away to the right. My last bullets hit his left wing. A large piece came away as if cut off with a razor blade. He too had had his fill. I did not have to pursue him. But there was yet another one. He had seen the danger and dived to the right. I followed him and was at his neck. After the first burst of fire his four machine guns pointed upward. The gunner had been hit. Get on with it, fire, fire, fire! But my ammunition had been spent. I had to let him go. With a long black smoke trail he disappeared downwards. I turned away sharply, back to the bombers.

The pilots of 264 Squadron had indeed suffered heavy losses, although it was not quite as one-sided as the reputation of the Defiant might have suggested. Despite the difficulty in penetrating the fighter screen to get at the bombers, the RAF fighters succeeded in shooting down three KG 76 Ju 88s into the sea off Manston, a fourth aircraft possibly being shared with nearby AA positions. The crew of all four bombers were lost and a fifth bomber from the 4th *Staffel* of KG 76 struggled back to base so badly damaged it had to be written off.

29-year old *Oberfeldwebel* Fritz Beeck from the 6th *Staffel* of *Hauptmann* Günther Matthes' II / JG 51 was making his second sortie of the day shortly after midday on the 24th of August. He had already crossed the Channel shortly after 0800 hours as part of the fighter escort for the first of the day's raids on the Kent coast. After lunch, he joined some of his colleagues from the 6th *Staffel*, together with others from the 2nd *Staffel*, escorting around 20 bombers which were attacking Manston. It's unclear whether these were the Ju 88s from KG 76 or the *Erprobungsgruppe 210 Jabos*, but at some time during this mission, he and his colleagues became involved in a dogfight over Kent with Hurricanes and Spitfires, probably from 501 and 610 Squadrons.

"Yellow 10", the Messerschmitt Bf 109 E-4 piloted by Obergefreiter Fritz Beeck which made a force landing near Manston on the 24th of August 1940. Note the oil staining on the cowling aft of the aircraft's spinner, caused by combat damage to the engine's oil system.

On his way back to Marquise near Calais, unaware that his aircraft had been damaged during this action, Beeck's engine began to falter following a rupture in its oil system due to combat damage. Unable to get back to France, at 1255 hours he force landed his Bf 109 E-4 "Yellow 10" in the stubble fields around East Langdon, near Manston. He escaped unhurt and was arrested by a local policeman who arrived at the scene just as his aircraft was sliding to a halt.

The next series of sorties from *Luftflotte 2* focused on airfields north of the Thames, with Kesserling sending a mass of Heinkel and Dornier bombers, together with both Bf 109 and Bf 110 fighters, across the Kent coast, heading towards the Thames Estuary. Keith Park was forced to put most of his available squadrons into the air to intercept the bombers, fearing they were again targeting his major airfields around the south and east of London. Anxious that the airfields of Hornchurch and North Weald would be without fighter cover, he called his opposite number in 12 Group, Trafford Leigh-Mallory, to release some of his squadrons to cover these two important Essex airfields.

While Leigh-Mallory didn't ignore the request, the manner of his reaction laid the foundations of a long-lasting and damaging dispute between the two AOCs of these neighbouring Fighter Command Groups. Leigh-Mallory initially sent Fowlmere's 19 Squadron south with their cannon-armed Spitfires, at the same time ordering three further squadrons to rendezvous over Cambridgeshire to form what became termed the "Big Wing" and fly south in order to make an impressive impact on the action over 11 Group. Neither action was of much help to Park's heavily-pressed squadrons in the south.

The Spitfires that equipped 19 Squadron were testing the practicality of replacing the standard armament package of eight Browning .303 inch calibre machine guns with the harder-hitting combination of two modified Hispano 20 mm calibre cannons. On paper, this was just what many of the pilots had been calling for to give them the ability to wreak more damage on the *Luftwaffe* bombers from greater ranges. However, the British technicians had not solved ammunition feed problems with the drum-fed Hispano cannons, with the result that ammunition jams were commonplace. Due to their size, the cannons could not be mounted in their normal upright position, instead being positioned on their sides using a modified ammunition feed system. The normal flexing of the wing structure during airborne manoeuvring, not uncommon during violent fighting, was sufficient to cause the undesirable jamming. When this occurred in both cannons, the pilot was defenceless. However, if one cannon jammed and the other fired, the imbalance of the recoil effect between left and right made accurate fire virtually impossible. The Fowlmere Spitfires had little impact on the day's outcome on the 24th of August because of jammed cannons. Eventually, the pilots of 19 Squadron argued that they preferred machines with eight Brownings since at least they would normally fire. In early September, the cannon-armed machines were replaced with older Spitfires from training units until the problems with the ammunition feeds to the cannons had been resolved. In reality, the introduction of Spitfires with cannon armament was delayed until the following year when the Spitfire Mark V started to reach front line squadrons.

The "Big Wing" took so long to co-ordinate and move south that they arrived over North Weald and Hornchurch long after the raiders had disappeared. While there may be some debate over how the request for 12 Group's assistance down south was passed on, it appears to have been a classic cock-up caused by Leigh-Mallory's lack of understanding of the importance in 11 Group for speed when intercepting raids. It became the basis of an ongoing controversy that eventually led to what appears to have been a disgraceful misuse of influence within the RAF hierarchy in the closing days of the Battle of Britain.

The next airfields on Kesserling's list for attention were the very airfields that Park had hoped would be protected by units from 12 Group - Hornchurch and North Weald. At Hornchurch, the remnants of 264 Squadron's Defiants were on the ground when the alarm was sounded and they scrambled as the high level Heinkels and Dorniers started their bombing run overhead. Having withdrawn from heavily-bombed Manston only a few hours earlier, the Defiant crews would have been forgiven for thinking they had somehow become the *Luftwaffe's* sole target. In the rush to get airborne, two of the Squadron's aircraft collided on the ground and another was shot down by Bf 109s from JG 51 and crash-landed back at base, with the gunner mortally wounded.

At North Weald, the airfield was hit by some 50 He 111s and Do 17s. Nine were killed and 10 wounded on the ground and the accommodation blocks were severely damaged along with the station's power house. The raiders that struck these two airfields retreated to France with little effective resistance. Keith Park was not in the mood to see his airfields left without the fighter cover that he had requested from 12 Group. He could ill afford for any of his airfields to be put out of action and he had probably already recognised from the intensity of this latest round of attacks that this was the prelude to more of the same as they entered the last week of August.

While the Essex raids were underway, *Luftflotte 3* was making one of its last daylight raids on the Portsmouth and Southampton areas. The radar plots of the 100 or so aircraft that were approaching from north of the Somme were unclear and the 10 Group controllers sent 609 Squadron's Spitfires in too low to have any effect. Portsmouth was bombed almost without any resistance apart from a heavy AA barrage from the city's anti-aircraft defences.

Back in the southeast, Kesserling decided that he would test the results of the day's events with a mass offensive sweep of more than 100 Bf 109s drawn from the units now spread around various airfields in the Pas de Calais. Despite Park's instructions to send the fighters up only when German bombers were detected in the incoming radar plots, a number of 11 Group's fighter units from Kenley, Biggin Hill, Gravesend and Hornchurch were all scrambled to meet the Bf 109s from JG 3, JG 51, JG 52 and LG 2, with the predictable result that both sides took heavy losses between 1530 and 1630 hours. Most of these encounters were over the fields and coasts of Kent which therefore witnessed the majority of the casualties at close hand.

In combat with Bf 109s over Folkestone, 32 Squadron from Biggin Hill lost four of its Hurricanes, all of which crashed or force landed around Lyminge and Elham. Two of the pilots were wounded and had to be hospitalised, but the other two, Squadron Leader Mike Crossley among them, were unhurt even though the second, Belgian Pilot Officer "Strop" Seghers, baled out into the sea. Two further Hurricanes, one each from 615 Squadron and 501 Squadron were also lost with one pilot injured as he baled out of his stricken aircraft. Biggin Hill's 610 Squadron also lost one its Spitfires when Pilot Officer Claude Merrick was attacked by Bf 109s over the Thames Estuary, crash-landing at Fyfield in Essex, from where the pilot was taken injured to Ongar Hospital.

The sweep by the German fighters was not without its downside for the *Jadwaffe*, with eight Bf 109s lost over Kent and the waters around its coast. Four others struggled back to France with varying degrees of battle damage, sufficient to cause two of them to be written off after landing. From the aircraft that were lost, three pilots became POWs, with four others killed or missing. Two aircraft from the 8th *Staffel* of JG 51 collided in the confusion of combat and crashed into the sea off Ramsgate with the loss of the two pilots.

Lying in the stubble field off Minster Road, Westgate, Feldwebel Herbert Bischoff's Messerschmitt Bf 109 E-1, showing the damaged left wing tip. The aircraft is surrounded by the usual group of police and LDV onlookers.

In a separate incident, *Feldwebel* Herbert Bischoff of JG 52's 1st *Staffel* had a lucky escape that afternoon.

I joined JG 52 in February 1940 and flew about 60 to 70 operational flights of which 20 to 25 were over England. I had just half a kill to my name – a Spitfire together with Unteroffizier Ignatz Schinabeck between Calais and Dover on 11 August 1940. On my last flight of 24 August it was a Spitfire that got me – coming out of the sun above me. He hit my engine which was then kaput. I was at 6,000 metres near London at the time. I dived away but soon realised it was impossible to get back to my airfield at Coquelles as by then even my radiators were kaput so I crash landed near Margate and became a prisoner of war for the next seven years.

Bischoff had managed to force land his Bf 109 E-1 "White 9" in a stubble field near Westgate-on-Sea. He emerged from the crashed aircraft unscathed after hitting an electricity pylon with the tip of his left wing.

The first day of the *Luftwaffe's* renewed offensive taught both sides lessons. The British lost 20 aircraft with 10 airmen killed, Manston was effectively out of action, with both Hornchurch and North Weald damaged. The *Luftwaffe* suffered heavy casualties, losing 41 aircraft and 46 men, but they had managed to pull off three raids without drawing the heavy bomber casualties that might have been inflicted had 12 Group got their act together. This meant of course that it was the fighters that suffered the heaviest toll, with 24 aircraft lost and 10 airmen killed or missing. Amongst these were as many as 16 Bf 109s lost or written off following the day's operations over Kent and the Thames Estuary. Both Keith Park and Albert Kesserling recognised that the series of rolling attacks undertaken by *Luftflotte 2* on the 24th of August had severely tested the capabilities of Park's 11 Group and the south of England's detection and control system. Worse was to follow as the last week of August passed.

After nightfall, the radar plots over the Cherbourg peninsula and other parts of France began to build up as German bombers started their first major night time assault on Britain. Until the latter part of August, the night raids on different parts of Britain had generally been piecemeal affairs involving small numbers of bombers, against which the only real defence was relatively ineffective anti-aircraft fire and occasional interceptions

by some Fighter Command Hurricanes and Defiants pressed into night-fighter duties, alongside the Blenheim fighters of the Fighter Interception Unit based at Tangmere and Shoreham.

Air Marshall Sir Hugh Dowding, Head of RAF Fighter Command during the summer of 1940.

This special unit was set up as part of Dowding's efforts to create a more effective night-fighter solution by experimenting with the cumbersome radar detection devices that were small enough to be accommodated in these twin-engine machines.

Formed as early as April 1940, the task of combining the potential of airborne radar interception with a gun platform that could interpret the information received and translate it into a successful night attack proved arduous and difficult. It wasn't until the end of July that the first night-time kill was achieved and by then, the Blenheims used had at best become a temporary stop-gap, frequently too slow to overtake some German bombers.

The answer was another development of the series of twin-engine aircraft designed by the Bristol Aircraft Company in the Blenheim/Beaufort series, the more powerful and heavily-armed Bristol Beaufighter. The first versions of the Beaufighter were handed over to the RAF for operational evaluation on the 27th of July 1940, but it wasn't until the 17th of September 1940 that the first front-line unit, 29 Squadron, became fully operational with this new type. This was followed in early October by North Weald's 25 Squadron, which had been operating the Blenheim Mk 1F night-fighter.

It was still a long time before before an effective night fighter force would begin to make its weight felt against these nocturnal intruders, a shortcoming that Dowding knew very well. He had lent all the weight of his rank to support the successful integration of airborne interception radar with a suitable new night-fighter, but it was not be a simple quick-fix. Getting the right answer took much longer than was hoped. As night raids increased, his lack of success contributed significantly to his eventual fall from favour within the Air Ministry, strangely helped along by the efforts of Lord Beaverbrook. The Canadian newspaper magnate had long been one of Dowding's strongest earlier supporters but with the start of a heavier German night bombing offensive underway, he used his influence to help remove Dowding from the head of Fighter Command, anticipating that fresh leadership would quickly produce a workable solution to the absence of an effective night fighter force. Dowding's earlier efforts to perfect the use of airborne radar interception installed in a new series of twin-engine night fighters were eventually vindicated, but too late to save Dowding or have significant impact on the Battle of Britain or the Blitz that followed.

The night of the 24th of August remains somewhat of an enigma since German bombers, on the face of it aiming for targets like Rochester, the Thameshaven refinery and oil storage tanks in the Thames Estuary, mistakenly overshot their planned target and dropped their bombs in different parts of Greater London. This was contrary to Hitler's earlier instructions, which had forbidden bombing London since he still harboured hopes that Britain would respond favourably to some form of peaceful settlement that avoided the need for risking an invasion. He was concerned that if London was bombed, the City's population would be less inclined to support a government that chose to negotiate an armistice with their German attackers.

Between 2300 hours on the 24th of August and 0400 hours the following morning, a series of bombs fell across a wide area of the City. Most of these landed in the dockland areas of East and West Ham, some in North London and others as far west as Esher and Staines. More central areas like Islington, Finsbury, Aldgate and Bethnal Green also took their share of damage from the bombers.

Hitler was not amused and became even less so when Winston Churchill used the pretext of the attack on London as the excuse to send some of Bomber Command's units to attack Berlin later in the week. Göring had assured him this would never happen, but it also showed that Britain was less interested in a peace settlement than he'd hoped. Perhaps the invasion would have to be treated with more seriousness – as soon as Göring's *Luftwaffe* had eliminated Britain's troublesome fighter forces.

25th August 1940

Fair weather during the morning saw little significant activity apart from reconnaissance, offensive sweeps and feints along the south coast. As the day progressed however, cloud built up along with the threat level.

A new realism had dawned on *Luftflotte 2*'s fighter and bomber units. It was clear that the attacks against England were nothing like the experiences they had enjoyed during the battles fought over Poland, Norway, Denmark and the countries on Germany's western borders. It wasn't just the physical and mental barrier that the Channel represented. There was something altogether more business-like and worrying about the way that Fighter Command had been able to respond so effectively to what should have been knock-out blows.

The main action of the day centred on the west of England where 10 Group scrambled three squadrons to meet a series of large raids that been building up over Cherbourg and the Channel Islands around 1700 hours. It was a comparatively small group of bombers, 37 Ju 88s from KG 51, escorted by over 200 Bf 109s and just over 100 Bf 110s. The British fighters were unable to penetrate this huge fighter screen and KG 51 managed to bomb the airfield at Warmwell, damaging two hangars and the station sick quarters. The *Zerstörers* took a heavy pounding again, with a total of nine aircraft destroyed or written off and three more limping back to France.

This was effectively one of the last major daylight raids on the West Country by *Luftflotte 3*, whose bombers subsequently concentrated on night operations over England. The bomber commanders in *Luftflotte 2* were demanding bigger and more visible fighter escorts for their daylight missions against 11 Group's airfields. The escalating losses among the fighters that this inevitably caused meant that virtually all the Bf 109s from *Luftflotte 3* were needed in the Pas de Calais. The *Zerstörers* were arguably less important, except to make up the numbers and cover the bombers north of the Thames, but it was the Bf 109s that had the performance to hurt Fighter Command if their fuel handicap could be minimised. For *Luftflotte 3*, this meant that there simply weren't enough fighters to continue the sort of daytime operations they'd been mounting since early July.

The late afternoon showed another build-up of activity over the Pas de Calais as a formation of bombers from KG 76 joined up with the fighter escort that would protect them as they headed towards Dover, Hawkinge and the Thames Estuary. More than 100 aircraft, including Do 17 bombers from KG 76 and Bf 109s from both JG 26 and JG 54, drew as many as 11 Squadrons from 11 Group into the air, but not all of the British fighters made contact either with the bombers or their fighter escort.

Spitfires from 54, 610 and 616 Squadrons were among those that did succeed in engaging the raiders, joined around 1900 hours by the hard-working Hurricanes from

Biggin Hill's 32 Squadron. Most of the action was over the coast around Dover, although some of the German fighter sweeps penetrated inland over Kent.

It was over Canterbury that 616 Squadron met the fighters from JG 26 and two of the unit's Spitfires were shot down. Both pilots were listed as missing, thought to have become victims of the impartial waters of the Channel. This indeed proved to be the case with one of them, Sergeant Thomas (Tommy) Westmoreland, but the other pilot was arguably more fortunate. Both Westmoreland and his squadron colleague, Sergeant Phillip Wareing, had intercepted elements of the German formation over Canterbury and, as often happened, they became so embroiled in the action that they ignored the standing instructions from both Keith Park and Hugh Dowding not to endanger themselves or their aircraft by pursuing retreating German formations over the Channel towards the French coast. As Wareing later explained in a letter to Tommy Westmoreland's sister:-

> *I was involved in a melee which started over Canterbury and stretched across to France. I saw four 109s in line astern and shot at each in turn, by which time we had reached the French coast, and 5 other 109s used me as a target practice. I had to bale out and came down on land. My German captors told me that another Spitfire had fallen into the sea in flames at the same time. They had sent out boats to search for the pilot. I can only assume it was Tommy Westmoreland as nobody has found any trace of him since.*

Sergeant Wareing had fallen victim to a number of German fighter pilots before the final attack by *Leutnant* Kurt Ruppert of JG 26's 3rd *Staffel* over Calais, which set his reserve fuel tank alight and fortunately blew him out of the cockpit. After being taken prisoner, he was entertained in the NCO's mess of the 2nd *Staffel* of JG 52 at Coquelles, before beginning his confinement in a POW camp. He had the good fortune to escape from his Polish POW camp, steal a bicycle and eventually board a coal boat going from Danzig to Sweden. He was later repatriated and returned to active service in 1943.

At 1820 hours, Squadron Leader Mike Crossley had led eight 32 Squadron Hurricanes from their forward base at Hawkinge to meet the raiders gathering over France. At 14,000 feet over the Kent coast near Dover, they intercepted a group of 12 Dorniers, escorted by over 30 Bf 109s. The Hurricanes tried to get through to the bombers and the inevitable dogfight ensued as the *Jagdwaffe* did their utmost to prevent this. Adding to the four Hurricanes that had been lost the previous day, 32 Squadron lost two more at 1900 hours that Sunday. Pilot Officer Jack Rose was shot down over the Channel, probably by *Leutnant* Ludwig Hafer of I *Gruppenstab* / JG 26, but the British pilot managed to bale out uninjured and, even more fortuitously, he was picked up from the sea after about 90 minutes. The other Hurricane was never seen again, and presumed also to have gone into the Channel somewhere off Dover, probably shot down by *Leutnant* Josef Bürschgens of JG 26's 7th *Staffel*. With sad irony, the British fighter had

been piloted by 19 year-old Keith Gillman who had been born and educated in Dover, close to where he met his tragic end.

Pilot Officer Keith Gillman

His photograph is perhaps one of the most famous of any image of the young fighter pilots that were defending Britain at the time. It was taken during the early part of August and for some weeks it featured in newspapers and periodicals as the archetypal image of the young pilots that were daily risking their lives fighting the Germans in the skies over southern England and the Channel. It remains an emotive image today..

Flying Officer Frederick Gardiner from 610 Squadron was also shot down over Dover around 1920 hours, but he managed to bale out wounded as his Spitfire crashed near Northbourne. Pilot Officer Mike Shand from 54 Squadron was involved in this engagement but managed to force land his damaged Spitfire near Birchington, walking away from the landing uninjured.

While 11 Group's fighter pilots believed they had inflicted more damage than is supported by the German losses that can be identified, the raiders did not escape without casualties. One Do 17 from the 3rd *Staffel* of KG 76 was abandoned by its crew over the Channel, possibly the aircraft that Mike Crossley claimed as having shot down in flames. The four crew members, two of whom had been wounded, were rescued by the *Seenotflugkommando*.

The fighter escorts suffered one Bf 109 lost and two damaged. *Oberleutnant* Heinrich Held from I / JG 54 was killed when his Bf 109 crashed near St. Nicholas at Wade, a victim of Pilot Officer Colin Gray of 54 Squadron. One of the damaged fighters was also from Held's unit, but the pilot managed to force land at Wissant without injury, possibly the fighter that Flight Lieutenant John Proctor from 32 Squadron had claimed as shot down over Cap Gris Nez. II *Gruppe* / JG 26 also suffered during this engagement, with one of the group's Bf 109s returning to Blecqueneques from this sortie and crashing on landing.

26th August 1940

While the north of the country was dry, dull and cloudy, it was brighter over southern England and the Channel, with high cloud and mild temperatures. More cloud built up in the west later in the day.

Luftflotte 2 intelligence assessed the results of reconnaissance conducted early in the day which still showed large groups of fighters on the ground at Biggin Hill and Kenley, targets that could not be ignored. Kesserling and his staff decided that the best way to lure British fighters in front of the guns of their eager *Jagdwaffe* pilots was to send another small formation of bombers across the Dover Straits, escorted by an overpowering force of Luftwaffe fighters. As the first instalment of the resulting series of attacks built up over Cap Gris Nez around 1100 hours, it was tracked by the ever-watchful eyes of the south coast's RDF stations. This large formation was later identified as Do 17 bombers from KG 3, escorted by Bf 109s from JG 3, JG 51 and JG 52. The 11 Group controllers sent 11 squadrons of Spitfires and Hurricanes to intercept the incoming formation well forward from the airfields on London's southern outskirts. As part of this reception committee, they also committed the Defiants of 264 Squadron from Hornchurch, still using Manston as their forward base for the day.

The British fighters mounted an effective defence over the Dover Straits and east Kent, effectively blocking the Dorniers trying to reach the airfields around London. Many of them were intercepted at 13,000 feet over Deal. Their bomb loads were jettisoned over Folkestone and other parts of rural Kent as the bombers turned for home, but not without casualties. KG 3's 7th *Staffel* lost three Dorniers into the Channel off the Kent coast with several dead, some wounded and a few taken POW. Another bomber from this *Staffel* limped back to France, running out of fuel and force landing at St Merville with two NCOs wounded. Two further KG 3 aircraft managed to bring their crews home, with one killed and three wounded, but both machines had to be written off after their return. Many of these casualties were probably the result of attacks made by 264 Squadron's Defiants, which managed to put in a number of claims for Dorniers destroyed or damaged before they themselves were bounced by the bombers' escorting fighters. JG 3 and JG 51 exacted their revenge on the cumbersome British fighters.

The Defiants attacked the German bombers over Thanet, claiming as many as seven aircraft destroyed, but three of the two-seaters were shot down by the *Stabschwarm* of JG 3. Repeating the claims made two days earlier, two Defiants fell to the guns of *Hauptmann* Günther Lützow, and one to his *Adjutant, Oberleutnant* Friedrich Franz von Cramon. Although some of the Defiant crews were injured, the bulk of them survived the attacks except for Sergeant Baker, Flight Lieutenant Banham's gunner. The pilot baled out and his unfortunate gunner was posted missing after the aircraft crashed into the sea two miles off Herne Bay.

The *Jagdwaffe* escorts worked hard to protect the bombers and suffered in the process. JG 3 was particularly badly hit, losing three aircraft over various parts of Kent, all three pilots being killed or posted missing. Two further JG 3 Bf 109s limped back to France to crash-land around Calais, with their pilots escaping unhurt. *Feldwebel* Adolf

Ziegler from the 3rd *Staffel* / JG 52 was shot down by a 610 Squadron Spitfire off Dover and rescued by a shore boat, seriously burned.

One of the more badly-mauled British squadrons was 616 Squadron which had only arrived from Yorkshire a week before. Their losses on the 26th of August highlighted yet again the risks of sending well-trained pilots without much combat experience to take part in the increasing carnage over the south coast. The big problem was the Bf 109s that were almost always over the Channel, Kent and Sussex, some plainly visible, but many hidden by sun and cloud high overhead. Return fire from the gunners in the bombers was also dangerously effective, a factor that many pilots ignored at their peril. Over Dungeness and Dover, 616 Squadron lost five Spitfires around midday, with two pilots killed, one wounded and one hospitalised with burns.

The Squadron's "B" Flight had been bounced by Bf 109s over Dover and "A" Flight put their Spitfires at full boost to climb to help their embattled colleagues. Flying Officer "Teddy" St Aubin was leading the flight with Flying Officer George Moberley and Sergeant "Dukey" Ridley in attendance. Arguably, they never saw the Bf 109s that in turn bounced them as they climbed and all three aircraft were shot down with St Aubyn the only survivor, burned as he crash-landed his Spitfire on the edge of Eastchurch airfield at 1215 hours. *Hauptmann* Josef Fözö of the 4th *Staffel* / JG 51 claimed the Spitfires of the other two pilots who were killed over the coast around Dover.

An interesting sequel to this series of actions began to emerge in early September 2010. One of the Dorniers brought down during the early afternoon of the 26th of August 1940 was flown by *Feldwebel* Willi Effmert. His was one of the 7th *Staffel* machines brought down. They had been aiming to attack West Malling, but his Dornier had become separated from the main formation above cloud and he'd become disoriented. His aircraft was then badly damaged by the British fighters, possibly 264 Squadron's Defiants, which had attacked the raiders over the Kent coast. He turned back for France but, with one engine stopped and the other damaged, he was forced to ditch on the Goodwin Sands, then partly exposed at low tide, with the aircraft flipping onto its back as one wing tip made contact. Wounded in the attack, Effmert and his navigator, *Unteroffizier* Herman Ritzel, survived and were taken prisoner, while their aircraft sank upside down into the soft sand, finally disappearing as the tide turned. The bodies of his two colleagues were later given up by the sea, one in Holland and the other washed ashore in southern England, later to be interred at the German War Cemetery at Cannock Chase in Staffordshire.

The sands have gradually shifted over time and divers found the remains of a Dornier bomber in a remarkably good state of preservation bearing in mind the intervening 70 years and the absence of some parts, probably recovered by excited amateur divers. A plan emerged to recover the wreck and bring it to a state of renovation where it could be displayed at the RAF Museum in Hendon. The Museum started working in conjunction with Wessex Archaeology and English Heritage to overcome the problems of a recovery in the challenging environment of the Goodwin Sands, the aim being to bring this unique aircraft to some form of display condition. No examples remain of this type of bomber which was the mainstay of German bomber attacks during the early days of the war and particularly during the Battle of Britain period. As with many projects of this type, doubt was cast on the viability of a successful recovery. However, the RAF Museum persevered with the project and through determination and appeals for donations from the public, the bulk of the aircraft's structure was finally lifted from the seabed on 10 June 2013, after several days of frustrating delays caused by the uncooperative wind and weather conditions.

The Goodwin Sands Dornier Do 17is finally lowered onto the recovery barge off Ramsgate on the 10th of June 2013 prior to moving to RAF Cosford.

Concerns over the potential deterioration of the structure when exposed to air after such a long immersion in the sea were partly mitigated by continuous spraying of the airframe with sea water. In order to preserve the structure while undergoing further examination and restoration, the Museum installed specially-constructed hydration tunnels at RAF Cosford with the aim of using a diluted citric acid spray to remove the accumulated salt and sea growth. This is expected to take some two or three years, during which plans will be crystallised to make the aircraft ready for its eventual display. The hope is that this successful recovery and restoration will fill a gap in the range of aircraft from this period that have been restored and put on display. What form this might take will depend on the safety and stability of the various parts of the aircraft structure once the hydration has reached its conclusion and all the accumulated sand, sea growth and marine animals have been removed.

137

As of June 2014, it remained impossible to determine whether this example of the Dornier Do 17 Z is actually the aircraft flown by Willi Effmert since the all-important data plates riveted to several parts of the aircraft and engines have still to be found. It's not impossible that these and other items of equipment such as the various machine guns and many cockpit instruments have been salvaged by enthusiastic amateur divers. Until proved otherwise, the assumption is that the aircraft recovered is Effmert's *Werk Nummer* 1160, coded 5K+AR. Surviving family members of both Willi Effmert and Herman Ritzel have been watching the progress of the RAF Museum's efforts with interest. By the autumn of 2014, the main part of the fuselage structure had been removed from the hydration tunnels and into the restoration hangar to begin the process of bringing the aircraft back to some state resembling the aircraft that crashed onto the Goodwin Sands at the end of August 1940.

Above Folkestone some 40 minutes later, it was the more-experienced 610 Squadron's turn to suffer the attentions of the mass of German fighters covering KG 3's bombers. Two Spitfires from the Biggin Hill unit were shot down, with the pilots baling out as their aircraft crashed and burned out near Hawkinge and Paddlesworth. One of the pilots, Sergeant Peter Else, was seriously injured and admitted to the Kent and Canterbury Hospital. A third Spitfire was badly damaged over Folkestone and Pilot Officer Frank Webster, its pilot, sadly died when his aircraft crashed in flames as he attempted to land at Hawkinge.

Half an hour later, units of JG 51 were still operating over Kent covering the withdrawal of the Dorniers from KG 3. *Major* Werner Mölders, *Geschwader Kommodore* of JG 51, claimed his 27th kill of the war. He probably shot down and wounded Sergeant Percy Copeland of 616 Squadron, who was later admitted to Ashford Hospital after force landing his Spitfire near Wye. He was not the last of the day's casualties among the newcomers of 616 Squadron. Pilot Officer Roy Marples was shot down by the Bf 109s a few minutes later and, after force landing his damaged aircraft at Adisham, he was also admitted to the Kent and Canterbury Hospital.

Another series of formations built up over northern France at 1400 hours as two *Gruppen* from KG 2 climbed to rendezvous with their Bf 109 and Bf 110 escorts over the French coast. The Do 17s of I *Gruppe*, under the command of *Major* Martin Gutzmann, were heading past North Foreland towards Hornchurch, on the north bank of the Thames Estuary. The other group of Dorniers from III *Gruppe*, under *Major* Adolf Fuchs, had already flown northwards, skirting the Thames Estuary and turning west off the Essex coast near Harwich. With North Weald perhaps the logical target, it was with some surprise that the 11 Group controllers finally realised this group of bombers had again turned northwest towards Debden airfield. Most of the bombers were turned back from their attack, but a few doggedly carried on towards the Essex airfield and caused not inconsiderable damage and casualties.

It was *Major* Gutzmann's formation that made its impact felt on Kent that Monday. Keith Park's controllers sent the Hurricanes of 85 and 615 Squadrons in to intercept the approaching raid. Off the Kent coast around Margate, they made contact with the Bf 109s of JG 52's I *Gruppe* operating as close escort around the bombers, with more German fighters lurking up in the sun. A predictable dogfight followed, with losses on both sides, including some of the Dornier bombers, two of which were shot down and two limped back to France, damaged but capable of being repaired.

After dropping bombs over Hornchurch in Essex, both the engines of Major Martin Gutzmann's Do 17 were put out of action and the pilot made a force landing some 25 miles southeast of Eastchurch. (Via Goss)

One of the two Do 17s lost force landed on the north side of the Estuary, coming down on Rochford airfield. The other casualty was *Major* Gutzmann's own machine which was badly damaged by the Hurricanes over Hornchurch and crashed two miles west of Eastchurch, with one crew member killed and the remaining three becoming POWs, including the *Gruppenkommandeur*.

The 2nd *Staffel* of JG 52 was hit particularly hard, losing four of their aircraft over Ramsgate and Folkestone. *Feldwebel* Alfons Bacher's "Red 2" was one of the Bf 109s shot down over Ramsgate and, instead of baling out and probably much to the displeasure of the club's members, he force landed at 1530 hours near the Club House on the Sandwich Golf course where he was taken POW. Two more pilots from the *Staffel* joined the growing ranks of POWs, but the fourth pilot brought down, *Unteroffizier* Hartlieb, was killed.

The Hurricane squadrons in action during this engagement did not escape without loss, with four aircraft destroyed and two damaged. Much to both Park's and Dowding's relief, however, the pilot casualties were comparatively light, with none killed and two injured. One of these was Canadian-born Flight Lieutenant "Elmer" Gaunce from Kenley's 615 Squadron, whose Hurricane was shot down in flames by the Bf 109s, forcing him to bale out into the sea off Herne Bay. He was rescued from the sea but admitted to hospital suffering from shock.

A yellow-nosed Messerschmitt Bf 109 E-4 taxies past others from I / JG 52 in their camouflaged blast pens at Cocquelles near Calais.

A final raid of the day was mounted around 1600 hours by *Luftflotte 3* units aiming for Portsmouth Dockyard, when more than 50 Heinkel He 111 bombers from KG 55 were escorted by a huge mass of fighters including Bf 109s from JG 2 and JG 53. Ventnor radar station was now back in operation after the damage that first occurred two weeks earlier, and the raid was successfully intercepted by four British fighter squadrons before it reached the target, with losses on both sides. Deteriorating weather also created problems for the bombers as cloud built up. It was finally time for *Luftflotte 3* to call it a day in terms of daylight bomber attacks in the west.

27th August 1940

Tuesday arrived along with rain and cloud over most of the country, reducing activity on both sides of the Channel. Over the south and the Thames Estuary, the cloud began to clear around midday and some operations began. The *Luftwaffe* focused on reconnaissance missions, with offensive sweeps by groups of fighters hoping to attract attention from what their intelligence group had convinced itself were the dwindling numbers of Hurricanes and Spitfires available to Fighter Command. There were comparatively few encounters during the day, apart from interceptions of occasional reconnaissance aircraft.

While the last two weeks had seen Keith Park's 11 Group suffering punishing aircraft and pilot casualties, the supply of new and repaired aircraft had normally been keeping ahead of losses. As these losses mounted towards the end of August, the availability of machines was causing more concern, but it was the availability of battle-ready fighter pilots that was more worrying for both Park and Hugh Dowding as the attrition over southern England took its toll. As with the *Luftwaffe*, which had encountered heavy losses among its experienced leaders at virtually every level, Fighter Command had also suffered dangerously high casualties among its battle-hardened pilots, particularly Squadron Leaders, Flight Commanders and other experienced officers.

Across the Channel, *Luftflotte 2* was already stretching its fighter availability to the limit in order to provide the bomber units with the growing number of fighters required for escort duty. With no real reserves to call upon, the only option had been to move more fighter units from *Luftflotten 3* and *5* to swell the numbers of fighters in the Pas de Calais. In the last week of August, seven additional *Gruppen* of Bf 109 fighters were transferred to *Luftflotte 2*, using bases around Calais and Boulogne. Nominally this should have added around one hundred fighters to Kesserling's Bf 109s, but in reality the serviceable strength in terms of both pilots and aircraft contributed much less than this.

Not only were there material shortages in terms of aircraft among all the *Jagdwaffe* units now ranged against Keith Park's 11 Group, but for some time there had been growing concern among the unit leaders that replacement pilots were arriving with very limited experience. Unlike the RAF squadrons where there was some opportunity for the newcomers to learn "on the job", albeit with high risks, the young pilots joining the *Jagdwaffe* units were normally kept away from operations over the Channel. They frequently operated as local defence units against British bomber raids which were targeting both the airfields around the Pas de Calais and Normandy, as well as the build-up of barges and other material in the Channel ports as the German Army and Navy prepared for the invasion of England, still planned for mid September.

Inevitably, this meant that the experienced German pilots were called on to fly more offensive sorties day by day, increasing the mental pressure that they were already suffering due to the risks of operating over the dangerous English south coast and the waters that divided England from the Continent.

From the information available in the *Luftwaffe* Quartermaster General's Returns, it appears that the period between the 10th and 31st of August 1940 showed the availability of operational pilots for the Bf 109s had dropped from around 85% of establishment at the beginning of this period to 75% by the last days of the month. By the end of August, the *Jagdwaffe* had lost (written off/destroyed in action or accidents) just over 20% of the strength it had at the end of June 1940, equivalent to 229 aircraft, or roughly double the number that the latest transfers into the Pas de Calais should have brought. In practical terms, taking account of lack of operational machines or aircraft under repair on the ground, this often meant that each sortie undertaken by a *Staffel* might involve as few as six or seven aircraft instead of the full complement of 12 or 13.

Both Park and Kesserling ironically had similar reasons for being grateful that the weather afforded some respite from the succession of losses suffered by each of the opposing forces. However, for Kesserling and his boss, Göring, the clock was ticking as the approach of autumn made the prospect of an invasion of Britain increasingly remote in the face of continued stiff resistance from Fighter Command in the south.

28th August 1940

Over most of the country, the cloudy conditions of the previous day cleared overnight, apart from in southeast England where scattered cloud persisted. It had also turned cooler with a southerly breeze doing little to stimulate the temperature. Inevitably with these improved conditions, the RDF plotters watched the now predictable build-up over Cap Gris Nez, preceded by the *Jagdwaffe* trying its luck over the southern counties with offensive sweeps by elements of JG 51.

Shortly after 0830 hours, inbound *Luftwaffe* formations crossed the Kent coast where they divided into two main groups. Between two main fighter units, there were about 120 Bf 109s forming the various escort elements for a small force of bombers. Some 27 Heinkel He 111s from III / KG 53 were surrounded by the Bf 109s of Adolf Galland's JG 26, where the *Stabschwarm* was accompanied by both I and III *Gruppen*. This raid was heading for Rochford airfield on the Essex side of the Thames Estuary.

A second group was made up of 20 Dornier Do 17s from I / KG 3, escorted by Bf 109s from I and III / JG 53, heading across Kent towards Eastchurch. *Luftwaffe's* Intelligence Chief, "Beppo" Schmid, and his subordinates must have had a thing about this Coastal Command airfield, since this was the third time the airfield had been targeted since Eagle Day on the 13th of August. This concentration on an airfield that had limited importance to Fighter Command's activities was to continue, with five more sorties being aimed at this target between the 31st of August and the 4th of September. Of all the airfields bombed during August and early September, Eastchurch was to receive only one less raid than the much more important and regularly-targeted Biggin Hill.

Keith Park's controllers scrambled three Hurricane squadrons to intercept the two groups, joined by the seven remaining Defiants of 264 Squadron. This Wednesday was to be the last day that the heavy fighter squadron would operate in the southeast before moving back to Kirton-in-Lindsey in Lincolnshire. The losses they had suffered during their week in 11 Group underlined how unsuitable these awkward, heavy fighters were to the heated daytime fighting over the southern counties. By the time the remnants of the squadron returned to the Lincolnshire fens, nine aircraft had been lost at the expense of six full crews and several gunners, with several further aircraft damaged.

The Defiants climbed at full throttle towards the Heinkels of KG 53, hoping to approach close enough to the comparatively lightly-protected undersides of the bombers to put their turret gunners in position to rake the formation from below. Adolf Galland was leading his Staff flight and III *Gruppe* as close escort for the KG 53 formation and came up underneath the unsuspecting Defiants as they were intent on closing with the bombers. *Oberleutnant* Walter Horten, Technical Officer in Galland's Staff flight, recalled the engagement.

> ....*a single Defiant which we approached from behind and underneath. It flew straight on for a while until Galland got closer to a distance of 200 metres (pretty close!) and opened fire. So did the Defiant with its quadruple backwards firing machine guns. I can still see the "corpse fingers" between the two planes as if it were yesterday. The pilot pulled his plane up and turned left and came across the front of my plane from top right to bottom left. I fired my first 90 degree shot with both guns at a distance of about 300 metres. I went in, fired the first burst of 20 mm too soon and watched the trail of bullets go behind the Defiant's tail. Quickly, I corrected and I could hardly believe my eyes. The two sides of the Defiant lit up as if it had been struck by a match and it plunged down like a flaming torch. I did not see if the two crew got out – I hope that they escaped unhurt as I had hit the tanks in the wings and not the fuselage. This lasted just a few seconds during which Galland and I were pretty busy and I couldn't see the two other members of the Schwarm. Oberleutnant Beyer must have been shot down at this moment by Hurricanes which were lying in wait, using the Defiants as bait.*

It was probably the Defiant that crashed in flames near Faversham, crewed by Pilot Officer Peter Kenner and Pilot Officer Charles Johnson, the latter being on his first operational sortie. Both pilot and gunner did not survive the incident and Horten went on to claim a second Defiant shortly afterwards, while Galland also claimed another shot down, his 24th victory.

This was the first of Walter Horten's seven victims during the Battle of Britain. A keen aviation engineer, it was Walter Horten along with his gifted younger brother, Reimar, who later designed the Horten Ho 229 flying wing, jet-powered fighter bomber that perhaps stimulated the more recent stealth bomber design of the giant American Northrop Grumman B-2 Stealth bomber. Both the Horten design and the B-2 bomber show a number of similar design features, most notably the absence of any vertical stabiliser surfaces in the bat-wing designs and the partially-shrouded engine positions. A partially-built original fuselage section of the Ho 229 is under restoration in the Smithsonian Museum in the U.S., having been captured at the end of the war.

From the *Luftwaffe* casualty returns for this engagement, it's unclear whether 264 Squadron had any impact on the bombers' progress. All the casualties the British heavy fighters suffered had been at the hands of the Bf 109s of JG 26. Certainly, they returned to Rochford a chastened group, discovering that their second Squadron Leader since arriving in the south had been shot down - they later learnt that he had managed to bale out with minor injuries. His gunner had also managed to bale out of their burning aircraft over Faversham, but had been killed. Their aircraft had been suffering technical problems, first with the undercarriage retraction and then with a blown fuse to the electrical circuits controlling the gun turret, not the sort of handicap you'd want when Bf 109s were on the prowl.

A flight of Boulton-Paul Defiants from 264 Squadron.

Out of the seven aircraft that took off earlier, three had been destroyed and three others badly damaged. Two full crews had been killed, as well as the gunner in the commander's Defiant. The squadron was moved the following day back to the base in Lincolnshire it had left a few days before. There, it was reformed as a night fighting unit and played no further role on the pattern of daylight *Luftwaffe* attacks on southern England. They were replaced the following day by 222 Squadron, a Spitfire unit that flew down from Kirton-in-Lindsey to join 11 Group's hard-pressed fighters, together with 603 Squadron, also flying Spitfires, which arrived from Turnhouse in Scotland.

The *Geschwader Stab* of JG 26 wasn't immune to losses. As Walter Horten suspected, the other *rotte* in the Staff Flight, *Oberleutnant* Georg Beyer and his wingman, *Feldwebel* Karl Stäub, on loan from the 3rd *Staffel*, were both shot down over Canterbury. Some suggest this was at the hands of the Hurricanes that had been sent to intercept the raid, but it's also been suggested that both of these had fallen prey to the Defiant gunners. Beyer, the *Geschwader Adjutant*, baled out of his doomed Bf 109, while Straub managed to force land his crippled "White 13" near Goodnestone at 0915 hours, and both pilots were interned as POWs.

Hurricanes from 79 Squadron had been scrambled to meet the raids crossing the Kent coast that morning. They had arrived at Biggin Hill the previous day to relieve the exhausted pilots of 32 Squadron that had been at the centre of the action over the south from the Kent airfield since the Dunkirk evacuation. Two days earlier, the eight survivors of 32 Squadron had landed from their last sortie to learn that they were being transferred to Acklington. They were finally bidding farewell to the Kent airfield that had been their home base for the best part of eight years. The newcomers that had come down from Acklington got their baptism of fire as they and the Hurricanes from Kenley's 615 Squadron tackled the Dorniers from KG 3 and their escorts. One of the 79 Squadron pilots was shot down and baled out into the sea off Hythe and two more were damaged by return fire from the Dorniers' gunners.

The bomber formations managed to remain largely intact, mostly due to the efforts of their escorts. Both airfields were bombed, with some damage at Rochford, but it was the Coastal Command airfield at Eastchurch that suffered most. Here, the airfield was cratered by bombs and two Fairey Battle light bombers were destroyed, but there were no casualties and the airfield was soon back in operation. While there were some recorded casualties among the aircraft of both KG 3 and KG 53 on the 28th of August, these were more related to take-off accidents and other causes, rather than from the attentions of RAF fighters over Kent and southern England.

Rochford became the focus of the second attack of the day around 1230 hours when the two other *Gruppen* of KG 3 sent some 30 Dorniers to try to put the airfield out of action. Despite the number of bombs dropped, there was little significant damage apart from some cratering of the area and the airfield remained operational in daylight, with night operations temporarily suspended.

A number of squadrons had been scrambled to meet the inbound raiders, including the tired remnants of 264 Squadron which could only put up three serviceable machines. Again, the British squadrons all faced heavy and effective defence from the fighter screen around the Dornier bombers, JG 3 being heavily involved in this action. Despite this however, II / KG 3 sustained three losses from this attack as the bombers withdrew along the Thames Estuary and over the Kent coast. One Dornier ditched in the sea off Foreness Point, where the crew were taken prisoner, all four having been wounded in attacks by various British fighters. This was the 6th *Staffel* Dornier of *Leutnant* Peter Krug (*Staffelführer*), which had been damaged by AA fire as it crossed the Thames Estuary near Southend, setting fire to the port engine. Krug extinguished the fire but, on only one engine, the Dornier fell behind and he saw no option but to dive and head for home. As they flew back east, he and his crew had the misfortune to be spotted on their lonely flight back over the north Kent coast by Squadron Leader James "Prof" Leathart from Hornchurch's 54 Squadron.

I sighted twenty-four Do 17s at 16,000 feet over Manston. I dived to make a head on attack on the leader but couldn't get him in my sights. Pulling up again, I found a single Do 17 going home. I gave it a quarter attack from starboard and enemy aircraft crashed into the sea off North Foreland.

Leathart's attack apparently wounded all four crew members, although one of Krug's gunners mentioned an earlier attack by a second Spitfire that he thought had been damaged by their return fire. The first British fighter had dived away to be replaced by a second Spitfire that caused all the damage. After ditching in the sea, the wounded crew managed to scramble from their rapidly-sinking bomber and they were rescued by fishermen and eventually taken to hospital in Margate. Two further bombers from other units in KG 3 were written off, with one crew unhurt and the other all wounded.

The escorting fighters from JG 3 lost three aircraft, all of which managed to limp back close to the French coast where they ditched in the sea off Boulogne. Two of the pilots were wounded, but all three were fortunate enough to be picked up by the *Seenotflugkommando* Heinkel He 59 rescue aircraft which were normally on stand-by during operational sorties, waiting to pick up airmen in the water. Two of these He 59 rescue aircraft deployed during the day from *Seenotflugkommando 3* were shot down by British fighters with one NCO killed and all the other crew members wounded but rescued.

The British casualties during this lunchtime engagement included two Hurricanes from North Weald's 56 Squadron. One of these had been damaged by return fire from the Dornier bombers and had force landed on the Isle of Sheppey, while the other crash-landed in flames near Herne Bay with the pilot wounded, having been set alight by the Bf 109 escorts over the Thames Estuary.

New Zealand's Flight Lieutenant Al Deere, had taken off with "Prof" Leathart and the remnants of 54 Squadron from Hornchurch to intercept the Dornier formation, but he was to have an uncomfortable experience that used up another of the "nine lives" he depended on for survival.

I had fastened on to the tail of a Me 109, one of three in close line astern formation, and was trying to close to firing range, when a Spitfire dived in from above and pulled around behind me. I clearly saw the RAF roundels as, fully banked in a steep turn, the aircraft was silhouetted against the blue sky. "Good, he's coming to give me a hand," I muttered into my mask.

Imagine my surprise to find that I, not the three 109s ahead of me, was the subject of his wrath. Before I could do anything about it, he had found his aim and I was riddled with a burst of fire which struck the fuselage and port wing, cutting my rudder control cables and seriously damaging the port elevator. One burst was all he allowed himself before breaking down and away underneath me. It was all over in a matter of seconds, but even in that time the 109s had made good their escape, no doubt encouraged by the support afforded them!

With only a slim chance of controlling his disabled Spitfire for a force landing, Deere took to his parachute over Detling while his aircraft plunged to earth below him.

He landed in a plum tree near a farmhouse, much to the displeasure of the farmer who appeared with a shotgun in case the pilot was German rather than British. It was his prize plum tree and he'd hoped for a bumper crop.

The last major incursions of the day by the *Luftwaffe* proved highly frustrating for Keith Park. Shortly after 1600 hours, six *Gruppen* of Bf 109s and five *Gruppen* of Bf 110s crossed the Channel towards the Kent coast imitating bombers with fighter escorts. It was a ploy that drew seven RAF squadrons into the sort of fighter versus fighter engagement that Park had been anxious to avoid. Such engagements inevitably meant losses for both sides but, at that stage of the battle, 11 Group could ill afford to lose either aircraft or pilots. It was a salutary lesson for the 11 Group controllers who realised that this engagement had resulted in relatively heavy Fighter Command losses. Four Spitfires and three Hurricanes were destroyed over Kent, but even more damaging, three pilots had been killed and five wounded.

After parachuting from his stricken Messerschmitt Bf 109 E-4 while under attack from AA fire and some Hurricanes, Oberfeldwebel Artur Dau from the 7th Staffel ./ JG 51 answers some questions from the local constabulary soon after landing safely.

It was again the newcomers previously based in areas outside of 11 Group who suffered the most. On their first early morning mission, recently-arrived 603 Squadron lost one Spitfire along with its pilot, with a further machine damaged and its pilot injured. Also involved in combat during the afternoon, the squadron lost three Spitfires and their pilots during the first complete day of operations over southern England, a sad testament to the intensity of the carnage over the southeast as August drew to a close.

The *Jagdwaffe* escaped with comparatively light casualties, losing four Bf 109s, with three pilots taken POW and one missing in the Channel. *Oberfelwebel* Artur Dau of JG 51's 7th *Staffel* had been lining up his Bf 109 E-4 "White 14" to fire at the second of a pair of RAF fighters that he and his wingman had been attacking, when his own aircraft was hit. He thought he'd been hit by flak, but it's also possible that he'd been the victim of Squadron Leader Peter Townsend, 85 Squadron's CO. In any case, he baled out and was taken into custody by the Coastguards, later to be driven to London for interrogation.

Prime Minister Winston Churchill had chosen this Wednesday to visit battered Manston airfield after spending some time mid-afternoon at Dover Castle, where he had been when the air raid siren sounded, giving him the opportunity to view the fighting over Kent for himself. As he and his entourage drove from Dover towards Ramsgate, they passed the burning remains of an aircraft that had crashed in a field close to the road near Church Whitfield. Firemen were in attendance, and Churchill was concerned that it might be a RAF fighter, but was soon reassured that it was German. It was the remains of a Bf 109 E-1 from the *Stabschwarm* of I / JG 3 that had been part of the offensive sweep that caused so many British casualties. The pilot, *Leutnant* Hans Landry, had been one of the few *Jagdwaffe* pilots to have been shot down that afternoon, baling out of his doomed machine over Dover, but suffering grievous injuries from which he later died.

Daylight faded on a day when the RAF had struggled to hold its own but had taken heavier pilot losses over Kent than on any day of the conflict so far. As night fell and the bomber forces of both sides prepared for their night raids, few were expecting the heavy attacks made by 160 bombers from *Luftflotten 3* on Liverpool and Birkenhead. While these may well have been aimed at the important dock facilities in those areas, they were a tangible reaction to the nightly raids that RAF Bomber Command had been making on Germany and occupied Europe, operations which had been stepped up a few days earlier. A total of 340 *Luftwaffe* bombers ranged over the whole of Britain during the night, representing the first stage of the night *Blitz* that was to gather pace as August ended and September began.

29th August 1940

Low cloud with occasional showers limited morning operations and persisted over the Channel coast and southern counties.

Soon after midday several *Luftwaffe* reconnaissance aircraft made sorties over the south and the Thames Estuary. Around 1500 hours, the RDF plots revealed a large formation building up over the Pas de Calais as Kesserling amassed another group of aircraft to continue his efforts to degrade the strength of 11 Group. On this occasion, he salted the gaggles of Bf 109s from JG 3, JG 26 and JG 52, not only with Bf 110s from ZG 26 and ZG 76, but also with a few Dornier and Heinkel bombers. Contemporary reports suggest that there were at least 500 Bf 109s roving around the twin engine bombers and heavy fighters. The whole formation was heading across the Channel, apparently on a track that would take them towards Biggin Hill.

Park decided he had to meet this raid in force in case the bomber numbers represented a serious threat and so 13 fighter squadrons were scrambled to intercept the raiders. As the Hurricanes and Spitfires began mixing it with the escorting Bf 109s over

Kent and Sussex during the next half an hour, it soon became apparent that this was another ploy like the day before. Park ordered the British units to abort their actions and return to base to conserve men and machines.

The newcomers from 603 Squadron were among those that made contact. They had learnt the hard way during the previous day, losing three Spitfires and their pilots, with a further machine damaged. This didn't stop the squadron losing two more pilots to injury in their damaged Spitfires before the recall took effect that Thursday afternoon. Both aircraft were damaged by Bf 109s over Deal, with one returning to base and the other force landing near Canterbury. There were no German casualties that came down in Kent during this time frame, although one or two came down in Sussex and the Channel.

Around 1915, a mass of Bf 109s from JG 3, JG 26 and JG 51 were overflying the Kent coast on another offensive sweep. This time, Park kept most of his available squadrons on the ground, sending Hurricanes from 85 and 501 Squadrons and the recently- arrived but already-blooded Spitfires from 603 Squadron to engage with the German fighters. As with most of these tussles between opposing fighter units, losses on both sides were inevitable.

JG 3 lost four Bf 109s over Kent that evening, with two pilots killed including *Oberleutnant* Flörke. The pilot of one of three Bf 109 E-1s from the unit that were lost had the good fortune to be rescued by the *Seenotflugkommando* when he ditched his aircraft in the Channel. A fourth aircraft from III / JG 3 crash-landed at Colembert heavily damaged. JG 26 lost *Oberfeldwebel* Graf von Treuberg from the 1st *Staffel* when his aircraft was shot down over Folkestone by a Spitfire. It's possible that von Treuberg was shot down by Pilot Officer Richard Hillary of 603 Squadron who had made his debut with the squadron on this sortie and managed to claim one Bf 109 over Manston, possibly damaging a second shortly after. Separated from the rest of his squadron in the excitement, he then tagged along with some Hurricanes that he encountered from 85 Squadron, and he took up the position of "weaver" at the rear of this group as they continued across the Kent coast.

While it's difficult from the surviving information to make a clear connection between attackers and victims in this type of engagement, it seems he may have then become the unlucky victim of a "bounce" by *Hauptmann* Rolf Pingel, *Gruppenkommandeur* of I / JG 26, who put in two claims for Spitfires he'd shot down over Dungeness around 1900 hours. Richard Hillary crash-landed his Spitfire near Lympne at that time, fortunately escaping from the wreckage unhurt. Pingel's other victim may well have been Pilot Officer David Pinckney, one of Hillary's squadron colleagues, who had baled out of his own doomed aircraft before it crashed at St Mary's Road, Dymchurch. Pinckney had been slightly burned before escaping from his Spitfire and was admitted to hospital. Other pilots from different units within I / JG 26 put in claims for Spitfires in the area, any one of which could have been the cause of these two pilots' downfalls.

Gravesend's 501 Squadron, perhaps showing the tiredness and fatigue that were affecting squadrons like theirs that had long been operating within 11 Group, also lost two Hurricanes in the early evening over the Kent Channel coast. One of the units that had been based in France before the Dunkirk invasion, 501 Squadron had spent most of their time since then operating within 11 Group, apart from a few weeks at Middle Wallop in 10 Group during July. They had moved to Gravesend on the 25th of July, where they remained until a move to Kenley in September.

Like the fortunate Bill Green on the 29th of August 1940, this sergeant pilot was rescued from the inhospitable waters of the Channel after being shot down.

Sergeant Bill Green baled out of his Hurricane into the sea off Folkestone and was rescued, while his machine crashed near Hawkinge. He is thought to have been the victim of *Feldwebel* Heinz Bär of JG 51's 1st *Staffel*, who made a claim for a Hurricane at this time, his seventh kill. 501 Squadron also lost the aircraft of Flight Lieutenant John Gibson, who baled out after being hit over Hawkinge, possibly the victim of *Leutnant* Martin Rysavy of the 2nd *Staffel* / JG 26. Gibson landed unhurt at Mill Hill Farm near Ottinge and his Hurricane crashed on Ladwood Farm, Acrise. Over the coast near the Kent-Sussex border, 85 Squadron also lost a Hurricane over Winchelsea and the pilot was killed.

That night, the Liverpool area took another hammering as 137 *Luftflotte 3* bombers dropped some 132 tons of high explosives and 313 incendiary canisters over the area. Such attacks would continue on successive nights both in the northwest and others parts of Britain.